THE PERFECT POWER
WITHIN YOU

Jack and Cornelia Addington

DEVORSS *Publications*

The Perfect Power Within You
Copyright © 1973 by Jack and Cornelia Addington

ISBN: 9780875161792
Library of Congress Control Number: 73-87712

Thirteenth Printing, 2015

DeVorss & Company, Publisher
P.O. Box 1389
Camarillo CA 93011-1389
www.devorss.com

Printed in the United States of America

CONTENTS

INTRODUCTION

In January of 1970 a dream of mine came true. It happened like this. A man in Walnut Creek, California, wrote me that he had been listening to my broadcasts and, as a result, had sent for some of my books. He wondered if I had any printed material that I would be willing to send to him to use in a class he was currently conducting for a group of convicts at Folsom Prison. In response to his request, I sent the class a number of my books.

"What else could I send these men?" I wondered. And then I thought of my Home Study Course, *The Perfect Power Within You*, a 10-lesson course in printed form that had been instrumental in helping thousands of my students chart a new life for themselves. I had just 50 sets of the lessons left and I sent them all to him.

Frankly, I was not prepared for the enthusiastic response of this group of convicts in California's toughest maximum security prison. Many of them had been on death row and were considered beyond help. I was, therefore, thrilled beyond words to receive letters from these men telling me how much they were getting from my 10-week, 70-day program for a new life.

The dedicated Chaplain who sponsored the

prison class wrote asking me if they could reprint the Course in the prison print shop for use in the prison. When I agreed, they printed 200 sets and distributed them among the prison population. The next thing I knew, another printing was in process, and we were able to secure copies from them to share with other prisons that had become interested in this successful rehabilitation program. It literally caught on like wildfire and soon classes were starting in many prisons.

During this period I made several trips to Folsom to speak to the men. I found that those who worked with the course changed completely. Something had happened to those men. I was particularly impressed by the way some of them had become free in their manner of thinking and speaking. Even under prison conditions, the men who attended the classes were actually radiant, their faces open, eyes shining. They were eager to share their spiritual experience, eager to help others find the help they had found. At the conclusion of my talks the men would take turns speaking. They spoke eloquently of the help they had received since they had begun to understand and use the Perfect Power Within. The change in these prison inmates became so noticeable that many were paroled early. The wonderful part of it all was that in a prison noted for its high rate of recidivism, the men who had discovered the Power within them *did not return to prison.*

If this material could be used with such great

success among a group of so-called "hardened criminals," why weren't we making it available to more people in the outer world? We'd seen the acid test. It was plain that it should be put in book form so that people in all walks of life might use it.

We are all locked in prisons of some sort, prisons of our own making. One of the easiest things to get into—and the hardest to get out of—is a deep mental rut. It is surprising how many of us wallow around in ruts. We want to get out but we don't know how.

Years ago when I was a praticing attorney I heard Dr. Ernest Holmes, author of *The Science of Mind,* say: "There is a Power for Good in the Universe and you can use it!" The more I thought of it, the more I realized that this was the pearl of great price. At that point in my life I left the practice of law to begin a new life teachings others to discover the Perfect Power within and use it in every day living.

In the 25 years I have since spent working with people, it has become evident to me that it makes no difference who a person is, how old he is, or what his life experience has been, an understanding of the Perfect Power within can change his life in a dramatic way. The Perfect Power within you is Universal Mind Power. When you become one with Universal Mind Power you become one with All-Power, drawing to you all that you need from the Universe. Once you have learned to let Universal Mind Power flow unimpeded through your life, miraculous things begin to happen.

This book provides a home study course that will take 10 weeks—70 days. If you will follow the 10 lessons, one a week, using the daily Statements of Truth, one each day, you will find that even before the 70 days are up, you will already be realizing your goals. Step by step, these lessons will lead you through a journey of self-discovery during which a mental transformation takes place. They provide a mental discipline without being tedious or exhausting. At the end of the 70-day period of following this program faithfully you will find yourself so uplifted in consciousness that you will consider yourself spiritually reborn.

After 70 days of sustained spiritual consciousness, the subconscious mind becomes cleansed of old negative patterns, the conscious mind having reprogrammed it just as one would reprogram a computer. Why 70 days? Experience has shown that 70 days is the ideal time to retrain the subconscious mind. Seventy days of persistent effort can build the foundation of a new life. By fasting from negative, destructive thought patterns and filling the mind with positive, mentally constructive thoughts and ideas, it is possible in 70 days to become a new person in mind and body.

If you had a pail of dirty water and each day you poured a cup of clean water into it, within days you would have a pail of clear water. The clear water would replace the dirty water in the pail. In much the same way, constructive thinking cleanses the mind of old, negative thought patterns.

What is YOUR goal? What would YOU like to accomplish?

Psychologists claim that the average man uses no more than 6% of his mind power. When he is able to tap the Universal Mind Power he finds that he is tapping an infinite Source. He soon sees that the use of Mind is the most important activity in life. Everything begins in Mind. That which we can conceive, we can achieve. There is no goal too great to be realized—family unity, business success, companionship, creative expression, prosperity or a physical healing. Change your consciousness and you change your world. Learn how to retrain your subconscious mind and you have the key to life. No one can ever take it from you.

So many lives have been changed through this 70-day program that I believe it is imperative to share this plan on a larger scale. So, here it is for YOU! Everyone desires to live a happier, healthier, more spiritual, more abundant life. This book will help you if you follow directions and stick with it for 70 days. No one can do it for you. It is up to you!

HOW TO GO ABOUT TAKING THIS COURSE

A Scientifically Planned Program

These lessons that helped the prisoners so much have been used in their original form by thousands of people in all walks of life. Some, before taking this course, considered themselves highly successful, others failures. Yet, all found that they were greatly benefited by the 70-day program. It worked because it had been scientifically planned to stimulate the mind to greater achievement and spiritual unfoldment.

Be Sure to Follow Instructions

Spend a week on each lesson. There are 10 lessons in all with 70 daily Statements of Truth, one for each day of the 10 weeks. Study daily until you have mastered the lesson for the week and made the Statement of Truth for each day a part of you. You will find each lesson brief and to the point. Do not be content to read it once. Read it over and over until it becomes a part of your thinking. I suggest you copy the 7 Statements of Truth for the week on cards so that you can carry them with you during the day. Look at the card for the day often; meditate on it, live with it until you accept it completely with the whole mind.

You will have mastered each lesson when:

1. you have read the lesson through often enough so that you know and feel it has become a true part of your thinking;

2. you have affirmed your daily Statements of Truth many times until they, too, have become an important part of your over-all thinking.

Many questions will arise in your mind. This is excellent. These questions answer themselves as you continue with your studies.

Repetition is Important

This is a workbook, a book of action, implementation and achievement. The Statements of Truth are designed to be read over and over until they become firmly planted in the subconscious mind which is the center of habit. It leaves the reasoning and decision making to the conscious mind. When the order is given repeatedly to the subconscious mind, a new pattern of thinking is established and the subconscious mind acts upon it. Through repetition, new and better thinking habits are born. It is just as easy, we find, to think constructively and creatively as it is to think destructively and negatively. In 70 days, through repetition of the 70 Statements of Truth, it is possible to so transform the subconscious thinking as to make a heaven of hell. Seventy days of creative, constructive thinking cannot fail to up-lift and transform the life of anyone entering into such a program.

This book is a training ground in which to learn how to remove the limiting thoughts that have shackled the mind, and open it up to an entirely new direction of constructive, prosperous and ful-filled living.

The Statements of Truth are powerful affirma-tions, each designed for a purpose. Be sure to use them as directed. Read them over and over until they are part of your being, deeply planted in your subconscious mind. Meditate on them until they sing in your mind. As each day of living with the thought for that day progresses, you will find the Statement for that day expand and grow like a flowering tree, and the tree will yield its fruit from then on.

Now you are ready to begin the BIG ADVEN-TURE because of this momentous decision you have made to discover and use the Perfect Power within you.

Jack and Cornelia Addington

Lesson I

DISCOVERING THE PERFECT POWER WITHIN YOU

You are now starting a glorious adventure that will revolutionize your thinking and change the course of your whole life. This sounds like a big order and it is truly that.

People are seeking peace of mind, serenity of spirit, and dominion over the life they are living. Even though everyone is seeking these things, they do not know where to begin. In the famous story, "A Message to Garcia," the man who was to deliver the message knew that Garcia would be found somewhere on the island of Cuba, and that was about all that he knew of his whereabouts. Using all of the strength, wisdom, and intelligence that he had, he persisted until he found his man.

In seeking to discover the Perfect Power within us, we, too, must use all of the strength, wisdom, and intelligence we have, and we must persist in our seeking until we find the real Truth about ourselves.

Does peace of mind exist for you and can it really be attained? Yes—it does exist and it most certainly can be attained by you.

Can real prosperity be attained by you? Yes—it most certainly can.

Can dominion over life be attained by you? Yes—it most certainly can.

You need not be controlled by the limiting circumstances and conditions that exist in your life today. Health, prosperity, and happiness are your true heritage. As a heritage, they have already been given to you but you have not claimed them. You have not claimed them because you did not know they belonged to you.

There is an ancient legend of a king whose first born was a son. This king wanted his son to love the people and to be a part of them so he could understand their problems, and be a true and respected leader. While his son was still an infant, the king put the child into the home of a peasant family and there the boy grew up thinking of himself as being a member of the struggling peasant class. When he became a young man, he was told the truth, that he was a prince and heir to the kingdom. Even though the king told the young man this truth over and over, it was still difficult for the young man to believe. He had to reeducate himself to think as a prince and a future king, as a person with authority and not as one who was struggling with the soil to eke out a bare existence. He had the power and the authority of the prince all of the time but he did not know it.

Your great kingdom is the kingdom of mind. Very few people realize what this means. They drift along, being buffeted by life, being dominated by the conditions and circumstances surrounding them, acting as peasants in a kingdom in which they should be king.

In this grand adventure of discovering the Perfect Power within you, you will find there are definite laws. As you understand these laws and apply them intelligently and wisely, your whole life will change for the better. These mental and spiritual laws are as orderly and law-abiding as the physical laws of the universe that control the tides and seasons, and hold the stars and planets in their courses.

As you use these mental and spiritual laws, you will assume control of your life and affairs. You will find that your life is not subject to chance or fate. You will discover that your success and well-being depend upon you and your awareness of the Perfect Power within you, and upon the way you use the Perfect Power in your life.

What is this Perfect Power?

The Perfect Power

Very few people realize that within each one of us is a Power that is perfect. Yes, it is flawless, lacking in nothing. It is complete within itself, infinite.

You think of your body as being limited in time and space, having a certain weight and height and moving about upon the face of the earth, usually within a circumscribed area. Physical evidence proves this to be so.

This is not so with the Perfect Power within you. It is infinite; it has no limitations. It is everywhere present at all times. It knows all things, is all wise and all powerful. Does this sound as though I am talking about you? Yes, but I am talking about the real you, not the limited person you have always thought you were.

The Perfect Power within you is Universal Mind Power individualized as you. No one has ever been able to understand all about mind. Some have had glimpses of the enormous capacities and tremendous power of mind, but since it is infinite no one will ever know all there is to know about mind. The more we know, the more there is to know.

The thing I want to get over to you is that there is within you a Perfect Power that has certain tendencies and is governed through law. Most important of all is that this very power is centered in you and is you. This requires a little explaining. Draw a circle on a piece of paper and in approximately the center of the circle put a dot. This is the way it is with each one of us. Each one is the center of the little world in which he lives. Your world has to be seen from *your* viewpoint. You are the most important thing to you in this world, even though you might like to think you put others first. Even when you are thinking of others, you are relating yourself to them in some way.

Now erase the circle. You have only the dot

left. You now are the center of a circle without circumference. By erasing the circle, or eliminating the boundary of your world, you enter into the infinite life of the mind. You find you are the center of an infinite life in which you can relate yourself to the wholeness of life without subtracting from or detracting from any other part because it is infinite, or without limit.

The Life of the Mind is the Real Life

Now here is the key to remaking your life. YOUR MIND IS THE CENTER OF YOUR LIFE. The life of circumstances, conditions, possessions, friends, the body which you use, business success—all are created through your thinking. Your mind controls your life and YOU control your mind.

This is the reason that it is imperative that you think only positive, affirmative, loving, creative, constructive, and right thoughts. That is the reason that with each lesson you are given a Statement of Truth for each day and why it is necessary for your development that you restate these statements over and over until they neutralize all of the destructive, false, erroneous, critical, and negative thoughts that have been allowed to make a home in your mind for lo! these many years.

In this first lesson, I am not going to try to explain to you how the mind works. I will do it in a later lesson after you have become accustomed to using the mind aright. Millions of people drive automobiles today who do not know the first thing about what makes them run. They know how to turn on the ignition switch, step on the starter, shift to the proper gear, and give it the gas. Furthermore, they know how to steer it, they know the rules of the road, and they know how to stop it. But they don't know what makes the car run.

So it is with us in using the mind. We are going to learn how to use it, and then we are going to learn something about what it is. When you think of Universal Mind Power, think of yourself as being an inlet and an outlet of it. Also, think of yourself as being one with it and that it is one with you. In other words, you are Universal Mind Power, being Universal Mind Power at your point of use. Someone asked Jesus where the kingdom of God was. He replied, *The kingdom of God cometh not with observation: Neither shall they say, Lo here! or, Lo there! for, behold, the kingdom of God is within you.*

The power of the mind to think, to remember, to create, to visualize, to exist eternally, to guide and direct your life is the Power that is Perfect, and this Power is right within you.

Who Are You?

We are not going to try to arrive at an answer to that question now. Before you finish these lessons, your will be able to answer this question for yourself. It is a very important question.

I will say this, however, that you are the sum total of your beliefs about yourself and about the world in which you live. Furthermore, when you change your belief about yourself, you will find that you will change. And when you change your belief about the world in which you live, you will find that the world in which you live will change.

All of the beliefs that you have about yourself and about the world in which you live exist in your mind. When you change your belief, the Perfect Power within you will act upon your belief and will cause your life to change correspondingly.

When Jesus said, *It is done unto you as you believe,* he was stating a law of mind.

Several thousand years before Jesus, a Greek philosopher named Hermes discovered this great law and stated it in this way: *As within, so without.*

Beliefs are established through thoughts. Therefore, when one uses a constructive, affirmative, positive, loving thought, he will establish a corresponding belief.

Emanuel Swedenborg described this creative action of the mind in his Law of Correspondences which states, in effect, that the material and physical life corresponds to the inner life of the individual. In thinking about who you are, may I

at this time state that you are not just a mere
man living a physical and material life, using an
intricate mechanism called the brain, but that
you are a perfect, divine, whole, complete spiritual
being, using the body while in this earthly experience. The Apostle Paul was one who understood
this and said, *Know ye not that ye are the temple
of God and that the spirit of God dwelleth therein?*
This will be difficult for you to grasp at first and
I do not want you to try. But as you grow in understanding, you will begin to see that you really are
the prince who did not understand who he was.
You will see that as you change your mind, you will
change your life. You will change your mind
through changing the beliefs that you have enter-
tained about yourself, and the process will be
gradual but sure.

Begin Where You Are!

You need not wait until you have completed
all 10 lessons to use the Perfect Power in your
life. There is nothing mysterious about it. This
lesson provides a simple spiritual exercise which
you can use.

At the end of the lesson, you will find seven
Statements of Truth. Write out each statement
of Truth on a separate card (a 3 x 5 card is suggested).

How to Use the Statements of Truth:

1. Relax and be still for a few minutes.
2. Now read the Statement of Truth through at least three times.
3. In silence, meditate on this thought for a few minutes.
4. Carry the card with you. Read the Statement of Truth and meditate on it as often as you can.
5. Read the Statement of Truth just before you go to sleep, and go to sleep meditating on it.

Have Great Expectations

During this first week expect to develop a greater spiritual understanding, a new concept of your relationship with Universal Mind Power, the creative source of all Good. Expect almost immediately to have your life and affairs outpicture this changed consciousness. I wish to emphasize — YOU have to do it. NO ONE CAN DO IT FOR YOU.

Eye hath not seen, nor ear heard, neither have entered into the heart of man, the things which God hath prepared for them that love Him!
                                        I Cor. 2:9

NOTE: This spiritual exercise begins for you the day you study your lesson. Do not begin to use the cards until you have studied your lesson. If you study the lesson on Thursday, consider Thursday or even Friday the First Day and carefully use each card. Do not use more than one card each day. They have been carefully planned to use as directed. Do not fail to use the cards. They are important to your new life. They will help you find THE PERFECT POWER WITHIN YOU.

LESSON ONE —

STATEMENT OF TRUTH — FIRST DAY

I Think Constructively

Destructive thoughts tend to destroy me and those around me. When I worry about someone, I do him and myself harm. Instead of worrying, I think, "The Perfect Power within me knows exactly what to do and how to do it." I trust the Perfect Power within me and within all of life.

And so it is

LESSON ONE —

STATEMENT OF TRUTH — SECOND DAY

I Think Affirmatively

Instead of railing at life and condemning myself, I now think affirmatively. Railing and condemning only tear down. Affirmative thinking builds up. I now look at the life that I live and affirm, "It is Good." I love and bless the Perfect Power within me.

And so it is

LESSON ONE —

STATEMENT OF TRUTH — THIRD DAY

I Think Positively

Instead of thinking of what a gloomy or wasted day this may be, I think of it as being beautiful and highly productive of good. This is a new day. I live today with enthusiasm and joy. I know that all things are working together for good in my life.

And so it is

LESSON ONE —

STATEMENT OF TRUTH — FOURTH DAY

I Think Right Thoughts

When I am tempted to think critical or mean thoughts, I turn to the Perfect Power within me for direction. It knows the right thoughts for me to think and I express those thoughts in my life. I praise the Perfect Power within me, I praise my friends and my family. I am one with all of Life.

And so it is

LESSON ONE —

STATEMENT OF TRUTH — FIFTH DAY

I Think Truth

Through the senses it is difficult to determine what is true from what is false. For ages men thought the earth was flat. It seemed flat. The Perfect Power within me knows all Truth. It knows what I don't know. I trust the Perfect Power within me to teach me the Truth.

And so it is

LESSON ONE —

STATEMENT OF TRUTH — SIXTH DAY

I Think Good Reports

I refuse to accept false reports about anyone. If I cannot say good, I say nothing. I do not think over any sickness, misfortune or tragedy in my mind. I turn my mind's attention to perfect health, good fortune, right action and divine love. I am grateful for this privilege.

And so it is

LESSON ONE —

STATEMENT OF TRUTH — SEVENTH DAY

I Think Peace

There are no thoughts of anger, violence or conflict within me. I turn to God and His Goodness within me. I agree with life and life agrees with me. I rely on the Perfect Power within me. I do not fear anyone. I am sustained in Peace. Perfect Peace is at the center of my being.

And so it is

Lesson II

HOW TO CHOOSE A NEW LIFE FOR YOURSELF

Whether you realize it or not, you are now experiencing your past choices. Your tomorrow depends upon your choices today.

Now I can hear you say, "But I didn't choose to have that cold!" Of course you didn't, but you either made a choice, or a series of choices, that brought mental confusion into your life resulting in physical congestion. Your body is a barometer which always reflects your mental state.

The Power of Your Choice

Choosing is the most important activity in your life. When we learn to make clear choices easily and confidently we begin to take dominion of our lives. Every choice is like facing a crossroad. Which road shall I take? Every decision is a choice.

Every time you make a choice you set in motion the Perfect Power of the universe for the purpose of causing your choice to become manifest in your experience.

George Washington Carver chose to help his people by finding many uses for the peanut which was easily grown in the South. Immediately ideas came pouring in to him from the Perfect Power within, which is Infinite Intelligence. Racial prejudice and other obstacles were swept aside in making his dreams (choices) come true. Even nature cooperated with him to make possible the most miraculous products out of the lowly peanut. He made milk and cheese, oil, soap, shampoo, rubber and plastic, leather dyes, and wood stains. If you want to know more about this thrilling story, read about this man who knew how to choose and let his choices become a reality. Through prayer and choosing to help his people, he became one of the foremost scientists in the world, and his people were warmed and fed, and factories hummed in the South through his efforts.

A choice becomes a direction to the individual subconscious mind which is one with the Infinite Subconscious which Gustaf Strömberg called the Soul of the Universe. Herein lies the Power. The subconscious mind is like a willing servant, never asking you why, never questioning your choice, but carrying out the orders you give it with unerring precision. Choose what you really want, for you will surely get it. Choose your thoughts carefully for each thought is a seed planted in the creative medium of life.

Freedom of Choice

Only man has been given the power of conscious choice. Only man is co-creator with God. This privilege carries with it a certain responsibility.

You must make your own choices. Your very happiness depends on it. You are a unique individual. Your needs—spiritual, mental, and physical, are known only to you. To let another make your choices can be disastrous. The Perfect Power within you knows what is right for you and will inspire you in making right choices.

Beware of asking others to make your choices. Letting others make your choices is relinquishing your God-given freedom of choice.

You must start now to exercise your freedom of choice even if you make mistakes. It takes courage to be free. The more independent choices you make, the stronger you will become. If someone else makes your choice, it is his inspiration, not yours, and hence some of the power goes out of it for you.

The Secret of Right Choices

Suppose you are convinced of the tremendous power in choice and are willing to be courageous in making your own choices. How are you to know if you are making right choices? They must be made in love and for the highest good of all concerned. This is not only for your peace of mind but, according to the law of reciprocal action, it

is that which we give into life which comes back
to us. It is the choices made with unselfish love
in accord with the will of God, which is Love,
that receive the Perfect Power. Ask yourself these
questions:

Is my choice good for me? for others?

Can I accept it freely?

Can I believe in it?

If the answer is "yes" to each of these questions,
go ahead confidently. You are on the right track.

Turn trustingly to the Perfect Power within
which knows that which is right for you and you
will receive guidance in making right choices. As
Jesus said, *When the Spirit of Truth is come, he
will guide you into all Truth.*

If you wholeheartedly approve your choice,
knowing that you have asked and received guidance in making it, you will be able to believe in
your choice.

Believe in Your Choice

Having made your choice, it is imperative that
you believe in it. Otherwise it will never come to
pass. Of course, you may decide to change or
amend your original choice from time to time but,
as long as you are believing in it, it is being brought
into manifestation for you. Everything in the material universe is constantly changing and so are
our thoughts regarding it. As we mature and ex-

pand our thinking, our choices will likewise mature and expand.

Beware of vacillating. As you can readily see, if you do vacillate, your desires will always be in process and never realized. Believing in the *seed* which you have planted, give it time to bear *fruit*. As James said:

> *Let patience have her perfect work, that ye may be perfect and entire, wanting nothing. If any of you lack wisdom let him ask of God . . . and it shall be given him.*
>
> *But let him ask in faith, nothing wavering.*
>
> *For he that wavereth is like a wave of the sea driven with the wind and tossed. For let not that man think that he shall receive anything of the Lord.*
>
> *A double minded man is unstable in all his ways.*
>
> (James 1: 4-8)

Choosing Establishes a Set of Beliefs

It is done unto you as you believe. Your life is an outpicturing of the beliefs that you have about yourself and the world in which you live.

A person may belittle himself. He chooses to belittle himself rather than to trust and believe in himself. He thinks that it is easier to escape by ducking under a cloak of shyness, unworthiness, lack of self-confidence, or lack of strength. However, that person is very unhappy and does not live a satisfying life. How much better to know that he can face every situation with strength and confidence, and to enjoy doing all things rather than thinking up excuses for his failures.

Many negative beliefs are concealed even from the self. Unfortunately they go right on outpicturing in one's life. Don't worry about these for they will automatically change as you are able to accept for yourself new, right choices. Be willing to let go of the old patterns you have guarded so long and let your life change for the better. Once you have chosen a new life for yourself, the Perfect Power within you knows how to bring it into expression through you. You will be guided into making right contacts. The people whom you need to know will be drawn to you, and all of the ideas necessary to your plan will be revealed to you from within.

The secret is to choose a new life for yourself and to believe in it more than in the old, limited, and unsatisfactory life. Say to yourself, "I choose to love the Perfect Power within me which always knows what to do and how to do it. I dare to choose what I really want in life knowing that as I steadfastly believe in these choices that they will become manifest in my experience through the Almighty Power within me. I trust in this Power and have implicit confidence in its ability to meet my every need."

Are You Making Choices and Not Realizing It?

Many times we make choices without realizing the tremendous power we are trifling with. *Every time you say "I am" you are making a choice.* This is the hidden secret of the ages. This is the most important thing you can ever learn. That which you associate with your *I am,* you identify with yourself. For instance, if you say "I am sick" you are literally making sickness your experience. Consider for yourself the danger in the following statements:

"I am always catching cold."

"I'm always unlucky."

"I get all the tough breaks."

"I am not very strong."

"I am always losing things."

You need not actually use the words "I am." As long as your words mean "I am" they serve the same purpose. Therefore, beware also of saying, thinking, or feeling, "People are always taking advantage of me," "I never meet the right people," "Nobody likes me" or "I've never been strong" or "I inherited a weak stomach," and "everyone in my family is allergic to something." Once you have identified yourself with one of these negative ideas, you have set the law in motion to bring you more and more of the same.

It is you who must select new habit patterns. It

is you who must make new choices. *No one can do it for you. The Perfect Power within you works through you.* You must create new molds for life to pour itself into.

Do It Yourself

This has been called a do-it-yourself era. Now I am going to show how you can change your life. You are the only one who can do it. Stop looking for things in the outside world to change. So many people think that if they can change people or change conditions, they can change their lives. They are sadly mistaken. They do not realize that when the people change, or the conditions change, they will still be unhappy. *All changes must begin within, with new choices.* Once these choices are accepted and believed they will produce a new environment and a new life.

At this point, take a sheet of paper and pencil and write down all of the objectionable things in your life. Do not be afraid to be frank for no one will see this list but yourself. Put down everything that is bothering you now, your own shortcomings, failures, and fears. Write down all problems with health, finances, and human relations. Be honest with yourself even though this list may seem negative.

Now take a fresh sheet of paper. It represents a fresh new life. Take each item on the old list and revise it to make a new affirmative choice.

Suppose your first list reads, "I never seem to be able to finish that which I undertake." Revise this statement to read: "I choose to complete each worthwhile project that I start. The Perfect Power within me is sufficient to enable me to finish whatever I start."

Suppose your first list reads, "I am a victim of asthma. I have had it all of my life." Revise this statement to read: "No matter what my past experience has been I turn away from it now. I choose for myself perfect health in mind and body. I choose to breathe easily and freely. The Perfect Power within me is healing me now."

Suppose your first list reads, "I am always behind with my bills. I never can seem to get ahead." Revise it to read: "I choose to experience the abundance of Life. The Perfect Power within me knows how to provide for my every need. God is my Infinite Supply and I have enough and to spare."

Once you have completed your new list of affirmative goals, destroy the first list. Let this act be to you a symbol of the step you have taken. You have now blotted out the old undesirable traits and conditions and have accepted for yourself a new course of right action in your life.

LESSON TWO —

STATEMENT OF TRUTH — FIRST DAY

I Choose Perfect Health

My body is the temple of the living God and the spirit of God dwells in me. The Perfect Power within me knows how to make my body function perfectly. As I choose wholeness in mind and body I am made every whit whole. I thank God for radiant health in every cell, tissue, and organ of my body.

And so it is

LESSON TWO —

STATEMENT OF TRUTH — SECOND DAY

I Choose Success

I now turn away from patterns of past failures. All of the Power of the Universe is mine to use. The Infinite Intelligence within me guides and directs my every endeavor toward certain success.

And so it is

LESSON TWO —

STATEMENT OF TRUTH — THIRD DAY

I Choose to Love and Be Loved

I am not alone. The infinite Love within
me is all that I need. As I give this Love
forth to all mankind, it returns to me as
perfect right companionship. The Love I give
away I keep.

And so it is

LESSON TWO —

STATEMENT OF TRUTH — FOURTH DAY

I Choose Peace of Mind

I find peace of mind through trusting God.
I give over every anxious thought to the
Perfect Power within me knowing that this
Power is all-knowing and all-powerful. As
I place my security in God, perfect right ac-
tion is established in my life and affairs.

And so it is

LESSON TWO —

STATEMENT OF TRUTH — FIFTH DAY

I Choose Right Employment

Today I am planting a thought seed for perfect right employment for myself. As I plant this seed in the Creative Medium of Life, all of the Power of the Universe goes to work for me. I am led to the right people and provided with right ideas. My perfect position is drawn to me now.

And so it is

LESSON TWO —

STATEMENT OF TRUTH — SIXTH DAY

I Choose Divine Protection

I am protected at all times and under all circumstances. God at the center of my being which created me knows how to protect me and guide me so that no harm can come to me. I have no enemies. I am one with all of Life. I am protected always.

And so it is

LESSON TWO —

STATEMENT OF TRUTH — SEVENTH DAY

I Choose a New Life

I forgive myself for all of the mistakes and confusion of the past. I wipe the slate clean and begin anew. The Perfect Power within expresses through me right thoughts and attitudes that produce right action in my life. I choose a new life today.

And so it is

Lesson III

CLAIMING YOUR DIVINE
HERITAGE

Release from Bondage

How can you accept a wonderful new life if
you think of yourself as a miserable worm of the
dust, or an unworthy sinner? Deeply imbedded
within man are hidden guilts and fears which often
keep him from accepting his good. These stem
usually from a limited, superstitious concept of
God. Alone, man seems to be powerless to rid
himself of emotional disturbances and blocks
which keep him constantly in bondage. It is only
when man is able to expand his conscious awareness of the true God and his relationship to Him
as a son of God that he frees himself to accept a
glorious new life. This new life is what Jesus called
the kingdom of God.

The Kingdom of God

There has been a great deal of superstition about
God and His kingdom. Somewhere, somehow, man
conceived the idea that the heaven which he

sought was a place, a city paved with gold, where he might live a life of ease in the far distant future. One was to sweat this life out, put up with all sorts of inconveniences and discomforts, that he might earn a ticket to this distant paradise. Had this been true, would not Jesus, the teacher, have told his followers where this place was? Instead, he told them that heaven was to be enjoyed NOW. He said, *the kingdom of God is at hand,* and *the kingdom of God is within you.* He taught that the kingdom of God is a consciousness of God-given dominion over the things of this world. It was to be attained and is attained today by *repenting,* which simply means the changing of the mind. The kingdom of God is still at hand. It is ours the moment we put aside our old foolish concepts and realize that God is right within us, expressing through us, and through this mighty Power we are *heirs to the kingdom* today. Now is the appointed time.

What Is God?

If God is to be found within us, what shall we look for? It is impossible to define God, but with persistence man can gain a larger and larger concept of the Infinite.

Let's see what we *do* know about God. The Bible tells us *God is not a man,* (Num. 23:19). As the poet, Tennyson, said, God is *nearer than breathing, closer than hands and feet.* He is your very life. God is All in All, Omnipresent, which means everywhere present in the same degree, Infinite. Therefore, God is within you and within all of life, binding it all together in One Perfect Whole.

We know from the Bible that God is Spirit, *God is Spirit and they that worship Him must worship Him in Spirit and in Truth.* (Jn. 4:24).

God is Love, and he that dwelleth in Love dwelleth in God and God in him. (I Jn. 4:16). Could anything be clearer? God is the Spirit of Love within you which, when recognized and called forth, becomes omnipotent Power, the Perfect Power in your life. Only by hating, resenting, and criticizing our fellow beings can we seem to separate ourselves from the Love of God within us.

God is Light, and in Him is no darkness at all. (I Jn. 1:5). If God is all there is, everywhere present, how then can there be darkness (ignorance) in our lives? Light means understanding, truth, divine illumination.

As Emerson wrote, *There is one mind common to all individual men. Every man is an inlet to the same and to all the same.* Plato spoke of God as *Divine Mind.* The Light shines through the One Mind dispelling the darkness. You are an inlet to the Divine Mind and an outlet to the Divine Mind, which is all-knowing. As Emerson went on

to say, *What Plato has thought, you may think;
what a saint has felt, you may feel. Who hath ac-
cess to this universal mind is a party to all that is
or can be done.*

*He is the Rock, his work is perfect; for all his
ways are judgment; a God of Truth and without
iniquity, just and right is He.* We find Moses sing-
ing this in his song in which he sets forth the perfection of God. (Deut. 32:4).

We are told over and over that God is Power.
God is my strength and my Power," (II Sam. 22:
33). Paul said, *there is no Power but of God* and
spoke of God as the *Power that moveth in us.*
Furthermore, we are told that nothing is impossible to this Power. This is the Power that we are
speaking of when we say *the Perfect Power within
you.* Do you begin to see your divine potential?
The Power is available to you at all times in all
situations. It longs to express through you the
moment you open the way by believing in it.

Once you know something about these attributes of God within you, you begin to experience
the peace of God *that passeth all understanding.*
Paul spoke often of the peace of God which he
came to experience as his own. He said, *the fruit
of the Spirit is peace, He is our peace,* and *Let the
peace of God rule in your hearts.* Paul experienced
this peace even in prison and when he did the bars
crumbled and he walked out a free man. So can
you experience the peace of God right in your

prison of doubt and fear and limitation. When you do you will walk out free.

But it was Jesus who brought us the feeling of the closeness of God as a loving Father. The Hebrew word for Father means *feeder, provider, protector.* It also means creative source and first cause. *There is one God and Father of us all,* (Eph. 4:6) making all men brothers. *Our Father* means our common Source, Creator of all, infinite Intelligence eternally abiding. Where? *in heaven,* which is the awareness of the Great Power within us through which we have dominion.

Who Is Man?

What is man, that thou art mindful of him, and the son of man, that thou visitest him?

(Ps. 8:4)

We are inclined to feel this way ourselves after we have glimpsed the glorious nature of God. It is only when we grasp our true relationship to God that we are able to claim our divine heritage.

Man is not just a blob of matter with a little spark of God concealed within him. Man is the expression of God. Man is God expressing as man, made out of the very Essence of God, for since God is All in all, He must create by Himself, becoming that which He creates.

In Gen. 1:27, we find that God created man *in His own image,* and Paul said, (I Cor. 11:7) *man is the image and glory of God.* We long have taken these statements to mean that God is made in the image and likeness of man. This theory gives us the anthropomorphic God, God in the form of man, a God with all of the limitations of man, with all of his weaknesses, foibles, and whims. This is not true. God is omnipotent, omniscient, and omnipresent, and man expresses God at the level of his awareness of God.

When we think of man in the image of God, it means that man has all of the attributes of God. Think of yourself as being Infinite Life, Infinite Love, and Infinite Power—divine Perfection waiting to be realized as you. This is a big step to take but one that will give you the keys to the kingdom. *Ye shall know the truth and the truth shall set you free.* This is that Truth and it will free you from your self-imposed bondage.

Man is to God as the sunbeam is to the sun; as one drop of sea water is to the ocean. The sunbeam is not all of the sun, but it has within it the warmth, the light, and the power of the sun. The drop of sea water is not the whole ocean, but it contains all of the elements found in the ocean. As someone has said, *man is the light that God shines through.*

Behold what manner of love the Father hath bestowed upon us that we should be called the sons of God . . . Beloved, now are we the sons of God, and it doth not yet appear what we shall be; but we know that when he shall appear, we shall be like him; for we shall see him as he is. (I Jn.

3:1,2). This was written for you and me. NOW are we the sons of God, and as God appears to us as Divine Perfection, we become like Him—Divine Perfection. The Perfect Power within us lives through us into glorious expression.

Jesus admonished us *Be ye perfect, even as your Father in heaven* (within) *is perfect.* Does this mean anything to you? It can mean a great deal to you as you live and express the attributes of God in your life. You can experience this divine perfection in your body and affairs—NOW.

Is There Good and Evil?

Since God is the only Power and the only Life, and God is Good, how can there be evil? *And God saw everything that he had made and behold it was very good.* Evil, so-called, is man's misdirected use of the divine laws of Life. You will see this more clearly when you study the next lesson on How the Law Works For You.

Men are now finding many wonderful uses for this tremendous power. It was atomic power that was used to destroy Hiroshima. Is atomic energy good or evil?

As we learned in Lesson II, man is given freedom of choice as to how he will use the Infinite Power with which he has been endowed. Is the Power good or evil? *Everything done in the nature of God, Love, is good.*

False Gods

What are YOU worshipping? The thing that you love the most is the thing you worship. Is it money, personal power, prestige, a diamond ring, a personality, or a Cadillac? Beware of false gods. I know a man whose business was swept away by circumstances seemingly beyond his control. He had nothing left to live for, and he wanted to end his life. That business was his false god.

Another man whom I know also lost his business, a large department store. This man believed in the Perfect Power within him. "If God in me can build one business," he said, "He can build another." Nothing daunted, he set out and succeeded in building a business ten times as successful as the first.

A politician built an empire for himself based on his political power and his own personality. He literally worshipped his own personality. He was defeated, destroyed. When last heard of, he was taking shock treatments in a sanitarium for mental patients. Hitler and Mussolini are examples of worshippers of false gods. All egocentric people worship false gods, i.e., themselves.

Contrast them with men who give themselves away in love to serve humanity. Their God is the true God who can never be lost to them. History is full of such people who, trusting God, proceed from one victory to another. Defeat never interferes with their progress.

Look into your own life. Are you putting business success, social prestige, or even bodily health before your spiritual life?

Jesus said, *Seek ye first the kingdom of God and his righteousness and all of these things shall be added unto you.* (Matt. 6:33)

He knew that if we had the conscious awareness of the Presence of God within, these things that we had spent so much of our time thinking about would be added. What a joyous experience that would be! No longer to worry or take anxious thought, but to know with glad assurance that God is taking care of us!

The Perfect Power of God within you is the answer to every human need. You need not be at the mercy of personalities, things, or circumstances. You can start today to live a life filled with joy, peace, and harmony, trusting in the Power within to supply your every need.

There is no person, place, condition or circumstance that can interfere with the perfect right action of God Almighty within me now.

And so it is

LESSON THREE —

STATEMENT OF TRUTH — FIRST DAY

God Is Peace

God within me is perfect Peace. I am serene, tranquil, and quiet. I am in harmony with all of life. The Peace within me is the Peace which passeth all understanding.

And so it is

LESSON THREE —

STATEMENT OF TRUTH — SECOND DAY

God Is Love

God is Love and when we love, we are like Him. Today I will let God's Love within me shine forth to all I meet knowing God is loving me through everyone else.

And so it is

LESSON THREE —

STATEMENT OF TRUTH — THIRD DAY

God Is Truth

God within me is Truth. I think Truth. I love Truth. I refuse to think falsely or critically of anyone. I know the Truth and I am made free.

And so it is

LESSON THREE —

STATEMENT OF TRUTH — FOURTH DAY

God Is Spirit

God within me is pure Spirit. Spirit is everywhere present. In Spirit I live and move and have my being. Wherever I am, Spirit is. Spirit upholds me, protects me, and guides me.

And so it is

LESSON THREE —

STATEMENT OF TRUTH — FIFTH DAY

God Is Life

God within me is Life. The Life within me is abundant, eternal, and complete. There is only One Life and that Life is the Life of God. That Life is my life now. I rejoice in knowing that the life that I live is the Life of God.

And so it is

LESSON THREE —

STATEMENT OF TRUTH — SIXTH DAY

God Is Light

God within me is Light. The darkness of ignorance, prejudice, and fear is dispelled by the Light of God. The Light is understanding and wisdom which illumines my every thought.

And so it is

LESSON THREE —

STATEMENT OF TRUTH — SEVENTH DAY

God Is Power

God within me is omnipotent. There is no person, place, thing, condition, or circumstance that can interfere with the perfect right action of God Almighty within me right NOW.

And so it is

Lesson IV

HOW THE LAW WORKS FOR YOU

What Is the Law?

The great poet, Robert Browning, wrote *All is Love and all is Law*. Browning knew what he was talking about. This one statement encompasses all of the Truth of the ages. It comprises, in a nutshell, what the great prophets and philosophers have been trying to uncover down through the years. What did Browning mean?

Love is the Power—law is the operation of the Power. Actually, it is Universal Mind Power in action. The great Law is that *for every cause there is an effect*. Likewise, for every effect there is a cause. The cause is not separate from the effect. They are two ends of the same stick. Every cause sets in motion the creative medium of the mind which produces an effect that is an outpicturing of the cause. Like produces like.

The Law of Sowing and Reaping

The Bible taught this law of cause and effect with such beautiful simplicity that even a child can understand it. It is called the law of sowing and reaping. The law of cause and effect is the law of mind in action but sometimes it helps to cite a tangible example.

The most common example is the farmer planting a seed. If he plants a carrot seed, he expects to harvest a carrot. If he plants a radish seed, he expects a radish. The soil does not reject the seed because it does not approve of it. It only knows to act upon it by furnishing all of the elements necessary to its becoming a plant. The farmer, who is the sower in this illustration, can aid and abet this process:

1. by planting good seeds which he chooses with care;

2. by preparing the soil to receive the seeds;

3. by watering and cultivating the soil;

4. by keeping out weeds which take from the growth of the seed.

So it is with us. Every thought or idea which we plant in the soil of the mind is bound to produce an effect exactly like the cause. The seed is the thought which is chosen by our conscious mind and is dropped into our subconscious mind. The subconscious mind is the soil or the creative medium of life. It draws upon the power and intelligence of the Universal Subconscious mind, being one with that Mind for all that it needs to produce its *plant* or visible effect. That is why Jesus said, "of myself I can do nothing; the Father within me doeth the works."

In Lesson II, we talked about How to Choose a New Life for Yourself. In choosing a new life filled with new, desirable experiences, you were choosing and planting good seeds. As you accepted these seed thoughts, they became deeply embedded in the *soil* of your mind. As you nurtured them with love and watered them with faith, they began to put down roots corresponding to the new patterns started in your life.

As you keep your garden free of the weeds of doubt and fear, you will further aid your *seeds* in their growing process. By the law of sowing and reaping, you will have a fine harvest at the right and perfect time.

You must, of course, allow time for growth. The Bible says, there is a time for sowing and a time for reaping and James was thinking of this when he said, *let patience have her perfect work, that ye may be perfect and entire, wanting nothing.* Beware of being like the little child who dug up all the seeds to see if they were growing.

Conscious and Subconscious Mind

Modern psychology confirms the existence of the conscious and subconscious minds. They are functions of the one mind. We individualize and use this one mind but are not separate from it.

The one mind which we all use is like a vast underground spring which comes to the surface wherever there is an opening. Consciously we tap this one mind or source of infinite intelligence as we think. Every time we think, we use the one mind at our individual point of expression. The brain is the instrument which the mind uses. Of itself it cannot think.

The conscious and subconscious functions of the mind are likened by psychologists to an iceberg. The vast portion of the iceberg is hidden under the water and only about one-ninth appears above the surface. The part that is visible compares to the conscious mind and the hidden portion is like the subconscious part of the mind.

The functions of the conscious mind are as follows: it directs, chooses, analyzes, envisions, imagines, and reasons both inductively and deductively.

The subconscious mind is subject to the conscious mind. It reasons deductively only, taking the premises given it by the conscious mind whether or not they are true. This is why we emphasize the importance of making wise choices. If your conscious mind tells your subconscious mind, "I have one cold after another," the subconscious mind, reasoning deductively, will conclude that is what you wish to experience and will set to work to produce the effect upon the body. The subconscious mind takes everything the conscious mind gives it, such as, "I am always tired," "nobody likes me," "the job is too big for me," "I'll never get a raise," accepts these directions as law and acts upon them. With the same unerring precision, it will take your affirmative thoughts and act upon them to bring them into your experience.

The subconscious mind never sleeps, but is on duty twenty-four hours a day—he that keepeth thee will not slumber or sleep. The conscious mind, however, is on duty only during our waking hours.

Because the subconscious side of the mind follows the orders of the conscious mind implicitly, it has been called *the willing servant*. It will never question the orders or directions given it by the conscious mind and has the ability to follow through unerringly in carrying out these orders. When we listen to it, it becomes our inner teacher, guide, and protector, and will give us hunches, intuitive flashes of insight which are invaluable to us.

Your subconscious mind is one with the subconscious mind of the universe which Gustaf Stromberg so aptly called the *Soul of the Universe*. Your subconscious mind is your soul, the sum total of your thinking, the collective record of all you have ever done or thought. It is the seat of your memory. It is your connective link with God and with all of life. Through the subconscious mind you hear the *still small voice*, divine intuition and guidance, and receive inspiration directly from

God which is Infinite Intelligence. Because of this, you need never ask another to make your decisions. You can be guided by the Perfect Power within you.

Cleansing the Subconscious Mind

Too often the subconscious mind has been thought of as a cesspool of dark, evil thoughts that must be cleansed by a slow tortuous process. There is nothing evil about the subconscious mind. It does have in it memories of past mistakes that cause inward anguish. Here we must become *the peacemakers*.

As you turn to truth and love, there will be created a feeling of compassion and understanding for past events and the people involved until eventually there will be no disturbing emotion when these memories come to mind. You cannot erase the memory, but you can change your reaction to that memory. All of the sting is taken out, *though your sins* (mistakes) *be as scarlet, they shall be washed white as snow* by love and understanding. We can replace our old negative patterns with new patterns of affirmative thinking.

It is like placing a bucket of muddy water under a faucet and continually running clear water into it, until gradually all of the muddy water is replaced by clear water. When we use our daily Statements of Truth, we are cleansing our subconscious minds.

The subconscious mind is the involuntary life or builder of the body. It continues to build and maintain the body in a marvelous way. It knows how to beat your heart and send the blood coursing through your arteries and veins and controls all of the other wonderful functions of the body. Consciously we are at a complete loss when it comes to the operation of the body, but the subconscious mind, through the Infinite Intelligence of the Universal Subconscious mind, knows exactly what to do at all times. Once you understand this, you can release the operating of the organs of your body to the Perfect Power within you with confidence.

If this is so, why does anyone ever get sick? It is because he has interfered with the creative process within him through stress, fear, anxiety, tension, or hostility.

Through prayer we change the mind, ridding it of these enemies of the body and thus let the creative process continue in its perfect way. If it were not for erroneous thinking of some sort, man would never be sick. The creative process within him knows exactly how to make his body function perfectly. We are not subject to fearful outer conditions. *The enemies are those of our own household.* In other words, there is no value in blaming your diseases, any more than your failures, upon outside causes whether they be germs, people, or conditions. You've either planted a wrong seed or you've let a weed sneak in. You should be in control of the garden of your mind.

Love is the Key

At the beginning of this lesson we quoted Browning, *All is Love and all is Law.* We have been talking about the law. We see that every thought we think produces an effect in our lives. We have the power to choose the kind of thought we want to think, and we know that it will be reproduced after its own kind. Are we getting the kind of effects we want in our lives? We want to be loved, respected, appreciated, needed, approved, and dwell in harmony with peace of mind. We want to live a creative, affirmative dynamic, healthful, and productive life. If we are not experiencing these fruits in our lives, then we have been plantings seeds not in accord with love.

Jesus understood the law of cause and effect as no man ever has. When he was questioned by one of the Pharisees, a lawyer, who sought to tempt him, *Master, which is the great commandment in the law?* He said so him: *Thou shalt love the Lord thy God with all thy heart, and with all thy soul, and with all thy mind. This is the first and great commandment. And the second is like unto it, Thou shalt love thy neighbor as thyself. On these two commandments hang all the law and the prophets.* (Matt. 22:36-40)

In effect, he was saying, "You must love the divine law of goodness at the center of your being with all of your feeling nature or emotions (heart), with all of your subconscious mind (soul), and with all of your intellect (mind). Moreover, you must love yourself as the image of this divine goodness and your neighbor (everyone else) the same way." This was a command or a must. And he went on to say (paraphrasing), "Upon these two 'musts' depend the right use of the law and this is what the inspired and enlightened teachers of the ages have been telling you."

The effects that all mankind desires to experience, in harmony with all of life, are only to be experienced through love. Hate begets hate, and each after its own kind, condemnation, criticism, resentment, jealousy, envy, and so on. *With what measure ye mete, it shall be measured to you again.* Do you see how love is the *fulfilling of the law?*

It is not enough to say, *God is love.* This love must be consciously expressed. You cannot take love for granted. *He that saith he is in the light, and hateth his brother, is in darkness even until now. He that loveth his brother abideth in the light, and there is none occasion of stumbling in him. But he that hateth his brother is in darkness, and walketh in darkness, and knoweth not whither he goeth, because that darkness hath blinded his eyes.* (I Jn. 2:9-11).

We must love the Perfect Power of love within

ourselves and within all of life to the exclusion of all hate, criticism, and condemnation of the self and others before the perfect law of life can be fulfilled to our satisfaction.

How to Use the Law Aright

Since the subconscious mind acts upon every order it receives, you can readily see that the directions or orders which your conscious mind gives to your subconscious mind are highly important. These orders become the law of your life. As you sow, so shall you reap.

Thus you may say, the successful man plants seeds of success in the creative medium of his mind. It actually is true that the successful man does not think thoughts of failure. He is not controlled by the rise and fall of the market and false appearances of so-called depressions. While fearful people fail, he succeeds because he thinks thoughts of success. Success breeds success.

You all know people who enjoy ill health. It is surprising how many diseases they are able to entertain. They regard themselves as suffering from tuberculosis, diabetes, rheumatism, heart trouble, and goitre, and confidently expect that one or all of these will get the upper hand any minute and put them in their graves. The more they worry over their bodily functions, the worse they become until operation follows operation and they are always miserable.

Contrast these dismal examples with the many healthy individuals whom you know. Healthy men think thoughts of health. They have no time for poisonous thoughts of fear, worry, anxiety, and criticism. They are engrossed in living life and leave their bodily functions to the great involuntary life within them.

What kind of orders are you giving your subconscious mind? What kind of results are you experiencing? This is the test. If you would like to improve your outer experience, start today to trust the Perfect Power within you. Give new affirmative directions to your subconscious mind and know that they will be carried out with exact precision.

A good way to do this is to take several good affirmations, Statements of Truth about you and your relationship to God, and meditate on them over and over until the old negative thought patterns are changed. Gradually, the inner life will become filled with peace, confidence, and a sense of power or divine well-being. As your inner life becomes changed, the outer experience will change to conform to the inner.

LESSON FOUR —

STATEMENT OF TRUTH — FIRST DAY

The Law of My Life Is Health

I realize that I know nothing about beating my heart or growing a cell. The Great Involuntary Life within me knows how to function my body perfectly. I trust Life and I experience perfect health.

And so it is

LESSON FOUR —

STATEMENT OF TRUTH — SECOND DAY

I Turn to God For My Every Need

Today I turn to God for my every need. I am supplied out of the wealth of His infinite Abundance. As I seek the kingdom within, all that I need is added. My good has already been given to me. I now accept it with a heart full of gratitude.

And so it is

LESSON FOUR —

STATEMENT OF TRUTH — THIRD DAY

Right Direction Is the Law of My Life

The Perfect Power within me leads me, guides me, and directs me into paths that are right for me. I quietly close my eyes to the outer seeming limitation and I hear the still small voice telling me what to do and how to do it, leading me to infinite fulfillment.

And so it is

LESSON FOUR —

STATEMENT OF TRUTH — FOURTH DAY

I Depend on God

To man this is impossible but to God all things are possible. I cease depending on my limited personality and I now place my dependence on the Infinite Spirit of God within. Of myself I do nothing, the Father within doeth the works.

And so it is

LESSON FOUR —

STATEMENT OF TRUTH — FIFTH DAY

I Am Expressing God's Abundance

I am come that they might have life and have it more abundantly. At the very center of my being is the abundance of God's life. I am expressing this abundance in everything that I do. As I freely give, it is freely given to me.

And so it is

LESSON FOUR —

STATEMENT OF TRUTH — SIXTH DAY

I Affirm and Praise Others

I affirm and praise the good in others. As I do this, the good that I affirm and praise multiplies a hundredfold. The seeming evil disappears. The nature of Life is good and for this I am grateful.

And so it is

LESSON FOUR —

STATEMENT OF TRUTH — SEVENTH DAY

The Law Is Good

Today I let go and let God. I bless the Law at work, that great Creative Principle which even now is bringing my heart's desire into manifestation.

And so it is

Lesson V

THE POWER OF SILENCE

Be Still and Listen

"For everyone who says 'speak, Lord, thy servant heareth' there are ten who say, 'hear, Lord, thy servant speaketh' and there is no rest for these," said Pamela Gray.

We learned in the last lesson how the Perfect Power works deep within the mind. It is there. It waits for us. But how can we establish communication with it if we are continually drowning it out with noise, confusion, and the sound of our own voice?

A friend of mine tells this story. She had purchased an evening gown for a special occasion. As the occasion drew near, she could not find the dress. She searched high and low. Her family searched high and low. It became the principal subject of conversation in the household and among her friends. She kept saying that she couldn't understand what had happened to that dress. One night she was awakened in the middle of the night. It was just as if someone had taken her by the shoulder and awakened her to tell her something. She sat up in bed, wide awake. It was as though someone said to her, "look again in your closet. It is in the bottom of your large garment bag." She got up at once and looked. There was the dress. It had slipped off the hanger and lay in a heap at the bottom of the bag where she would never have thought to look. She laughed aloud. "God had to wake me in the middle of the night to tell me where it was," she said. "I was so busy talking that I couldn't hear Him any other time."

Have you lost something? Try asking the Perfect Power within you in the quiet of your meditation to tell you where it is. Nothing is ever lost in the one mind, and the infinite Intelligence will tell you *if you will be still long enough to listen.*

When we become still enough to listen, God speaks to us as constructive and affirmative thoughts, dynamic ideas, divine guidance, and creative inspiration. *Man does not live by bread alone, but by every word that proceedeth out of the mouth of God.* (Matt. 4:4) The divine ideas of which we have been speaking are our spiritual food, and they are received in the mind which is *the mouth of God.*

Now do you see how important it is to turn off the outer clamor long enough to listen? It would be far better to miss three meals a day than to miss one's spiritual nourishment received in the quiet of the mind from the Perfect Power within. It is during these quiet periods that the real work takes place. Everything in our world today is the outpicturing of an idea that was first conceived in the quiet of the mind. It is here in the mind that the formless begins to take form, calling to it all of the latent power of the universe to bring it into manifestation. We see the outer activity long after the wheels have been set in motion by the creative activity of mind.

Chaos is Destructive

This may sound negative but it is highly important that we face it. The mental institutions are filled today with people who did not take time to be still and listen. People are gobbling up tranquilizers today by the millions because they did not take time to *be still and listen.* People are deteriorating physically today because of stress and strain that could have been avoided had they taken time to *be still and listen.*

Oh, the tragedy of it! According to the divine plan, we are meant to go within for our inspiration and then to live it forth easily, harmoniously, without strain or anxious thought. Instead, the people of today demand a constant outer stimulus.

Picture the average day of an average man. He gets up to the disturbing din of an alarm clock. From that moment on his entire day is filled with noise, hurry, and confusion. Usually he turns on the radio to catch the morning news, filled with disaster, disease and despair, and other tension-provoking announcements. As he comes downstairs, the television greets him. Junior is catching the first program of the day and mother is shouting instructions over the din. The father gulps his breakfast and hurries off, turning on the radio as he starts his car. Conversation starts the moment he enters the office and continues amid the clatter of office machines all day. Television or some other entertainment keeps his evening equally noisy. *Where is the house that ye build to me, and where is the place of my rest,* saith the Lord. Silence is so rare, in fact, that in our present-day society even a few moments of silence is referred to as "embarrassing silence" or "deadly silence." We feel that we must hold up our end of the conversation at all times and so talk much of the time when we have nothing to say. Even when we do have opportunities for quiet, there is the tendency to use that time for worry, reliving unpleasant events, "what should I have said there," etc., or just general squirrel-cage thinking.

All of this confused thinking produces chaotic living and is truly destructive to mind and body.

How to Discipline the Mind

This is the most valuable thing we can ever learn. It is far more valuable than periodic rest cures interspersed with months of restless living. It is the best insurance against nervous breakdowns, or other mental ills.

We cultivate an inner peace by making our peace with outer circumstances. It is important to start each day with a period of meditation and reading spiritual literature, even if it is only ten minutes long. At this time we turn our attention away from ourselves and our problems, and think about spiritual things. It is the most important part of the day and should never be slighted. The longer one can spend at it, the greater use he has of the Perfect Power within during the day. Once having found this peace within, the secret is to take it with you wherever you go. If for any reason one finds himself losing his poise and inner peace because of outside circumstances, he should take the time to again find a quiet spot, even if the bathroom is the only available place to be alone, and commune with the Perfect Power within which knows what to do in every circumstance, and is always available to us.

The thing to which you give your attention, you become. In this busy, noisy world today there is no way to stop the activity around us, but we can choose our reaction to it.

I will rejoice that from all tormenting we can retreat always upon the Invisible Heart, upon the Celestial Love, and that not to be soothed merely, but to be replenished, not to be compensated, but to receive power to make all things new.

—Ralph Waldo Emerson, from a letter.

We do not have to become embroiled in other people's tantrums, irritations, and distractions, or in the world of outer circumstances, but at all times use the will to keep our attention fixed upon the blessed peace within. Your mind is your kingdom, and there you are ruler. You choose how you think and how you react to life. It doesn't matter what's done to you, it's how you take it. Mass anxiety may be contageous but one can build up an immunity to it.

Keep It to Yourself and Do It

Have you ever had a wonderful idea that seemed to lift you and take you soaring to a new height? You could see wonderful possibilities and a whole new future contained in this idea. And then you enthusiastically told it to your best friend. His face remained immobile. Somehow or other, he caught none of your enthusiasm. When he had heard you out, he said, "We-e-ll, I doubt if that would work." He had several reasons for his dubious attitude and, by this time, you had your doubts, too. It may have been a good idea once. It wasn't any more. But some time later you picked up a paper and read where someone had patented an invention and made a fortune on the same idea you had.

The power of a steam engine is caused by controlled pressure. The power in your idea is controlled by keeping the idea to yourself until it has built up enough momentum to carry itself into manifestation. Don't let the steam off. The longer you can keep it to yourself, the stronger it gets. Do not expose your immature ideas to be smothered by other people's negative opinions.

Every God-inspired idea (these come during your precious periods of silence) draws to it all that it needs to bring it into realization. Talk it over with the Perfect Power within you. It will give you right judgment.

Enter into the Closet and Shut the Door

When thou prayest, enter into thy closet, and when thou hast shut thy door, pray to thy Father which is in secret; and thy Father which seest in secret shall reward thee openly.
—Jesus.

The closet is the privacy of the mind. We are to shut the door upon outside turmoil and confusion, and *then* we are to talk it over with the Perfect Power within us. That warm, loving, infinite Intelligence which knows all and sees all, and is always able to direct and guide and inspire. Here, in the secret of the mind, we let our need be known (pray) and the Perfect Power within (Father), which sees and hears right here in the secret of our minds, will reward us or answer our prayer so that all can see. We alone know when the real, creative act took place when it was conceived in the mind in prayer. When the world sees our reward, or the birth of the effect in the outer experience, it sees in delayed action what we have already experienced within. So sure is the metaphysician that his prayer has already been answered that the appearance of the answer in form becomes almost an anticlimax.

Suppose a problem of health is troubling you. How do you go about talking to the Father in secret? When we go into the closet of the mind, we do not take the problem with us because that is not what we are going to discuss with God. We are going to talk to God about perfect health. Our conversation with God (and that is what every prayer is) is going to go something like this:

Infinite Father, I know that all things are possible to You. I know that You have created me as a divine, perfect, spiritual being, made in Your image and likeness, which is Perfect. I now claim this perfection in body, mind, and spirit. I accept health, I give thanks for it, and I accept the manifestation of health in my body.

And so it is

Be Still and Know

BE STILL and know that I am God. Ps. 46:10
Be still and know that I am the Perfect Power within you.
Be still and know that I am eternal life living as you.

*Be still and know that I am divine love
    expressing in you.*
*Be still and know that I am the fullness of joy
    within you.*
*Be still and know that I am heavenly peace
    within you.*
*Be still and know that I am the light of truth
    within you.*
*Be still and know that I am God and there is
    none beside me.*

And so it is

This is the power of the silence. Enter into it
with peace and thanksgiving. The rewards are
beyond all measure.

LESSON FIVE —

STATEMENT OF TRUTH — FIRST DAY

I say no man has ever yet
been half devout enough,
None has ever yet adored or
worshipped half enough
None has begun to think how
divine he himself is,
and how certain the future is.
—Walt Whitman

Today I contemplate my divinity. I worship the Father within and know that my future is certain.

And so it is

LESSON FIVE —

STATEMENT OF TRUTH — SECOND DAY

A man can receive nothing except it
be given him from heaven. Jn. 3:27

A man can receive nothing in the outer experience except he first find it within the silence of his mind. Today I find my heaven within where it is the Father's good pleasure to give me the Kingdom.

And so it is

LESSON FIVE —

STATEMENT OF TRUTH — THIRD DAY

All that you have within you, all that your nature so specifically fits you for — that or the counterpart of it waits embedded in the great Whole for you. It will surely come to you.

—Edward Carpenter

I now do the work at hand for which I am specifically fitted, and lovingly release my hopes and dreams to the Perfect Power within.

And so it is

LESSON FIVE —

STATEMENT OF TRUTH — FOURTH DAY

Prayer is the contemplation of the facts of life from the highest point of view. It is the soliloquy of a beholding and jubilant soul. It is the Spirit of God pronouncing his works good.

—Emerson

In the silence of the mind, I behold the Truth of my own being. I am one with the Spirit of God and His works are good.

And so it is

LESSON FIVE —

STATEMENT OF TRUTH — FIFTH DAY

Be able to be alone. Lose not the advantage of solitude . . . But delight to be alone and single with Omnipresency. Life is a pure flame and we live by an invisible sun within us.

—Sir Thomas Browne, 1605-1682

Today I rejoice in the advantage of solitude. Here I find my inner peace. I take it with me wherever I go. I let nothing disturb me. My attention is centered in Peace.

And so it is

LESSON FIVE —

STATEMENT OF TRUTH — SIXTH DAY

A flower more sacred than far-seen success
Perfumes my solitary path; I find
Sweet compensation in my humbleness,
And reap the harvest of a quiet mind.

—Trowbridge

I choose to have a quiet mind. I will let the storms rage without. They shall not enter my heart. I let God rule my heart and mind, and I am at peace.

And so it is

LESSON FIVE —

STATEMENT OF TRUTH — SEVENTH DAY

The mind is its own place and in itself
Can make a heaven of hell, a hell of heaven.
              —Milton, Paradise Lost

Today I choose to live in the Kingdom of
Heaven within. As I turn from the discord
and ugliness in my world of appearances
and remain true to the Perfection of my
Heaven within, I bring Perfection into my
world.

                              And so it is

Lesson VI

THE KEY TO THE PERFECT POWER WITHIN

Spiritual Mind Treatment

Spiritual mind treatment is the open door to a new life. Through spiritual mind treatment *we* become in tune with God. The Perfect Power within and around us ever desires to express the fullness of life through us. Spiritual mind treatment is actually our means of communication with God. It is receiving the word of God that it may be made manifest in our lives.

What It Is

Spiritual mind treatment is an orderly process of clear thinking through which the mind is cleansed of doubt, fear, and negation, and an entirely new pattern of thinking is introduced consisting of affirmative, constructive thoughts which recognize the Perfect Power within as the Source of all life and good. To the degree that the one treating accepts the new pattern of thinking, there

85

is a proportionate realization of good in the outer experience.

Spiritual mind treatment is scientific prayer. The reason we call it treatment rather than prayer is to get entirely away from some of the popular misconceptions of prayer. Treatment is not begging God or telling God. It is not a superstitious or supernatural act. It need not be done in any certain place or position, such as in a church or on the knees. No intercessors, saints, priests, or specially qualified individuals are required.

We have as direct a contact with God as Jesus did if we knew it. Prayer has long been thought of as petitioning an erratic or capricious power outside of the self, a power that may hear one minute and not the next, or may reward one and punish another. The Perfect Power within is available to all at all times in the same degree—infinite.

It is the Father's good pleasure to give you the Kingdom. Your Father knoweth ye have need of these things. Ask, and it shall be given you; seek, and ye shall find; knock, and it shall be opened unto you: For every one that asketh receiveth; and he that seeketh findeth; and to him that knocketh it shall be opened. Jesus.

Every Prayer Receives an Answer

"Ye ask, and receive not, because ye ask amiss." (James 4.3). Every treatment that would take from or hurt another is not according to the nature

of God and is therefore asking *amiss.* You will receive an answer—you will draw the hurt unto yourself. It is the law of life that *as you mete, it shall be meted to you again.* If you do not believe in your treatment, if you have no faith, you will, of course, receive exactly what you expect, *as thou hast believed, so be it done unto thee.*

When your treatment is motivated by love it becomes the key to the Perfect Power within and the answer is right for you and for everyone.

Spiritual Mind Treatment Never Fails!

All things are possible to the Perfect Power within you. Through spiritual mind treatment all manner of sickness is healed, mental confusion is clarified, and peace of mind is established. All problems become answers. Guidance is given in making decisions, harmony is established in human relations and the answer is found to every human need.

The technique I am about to give you is the most valuable thing you can ever learn. Never again need you stand and wring your hands in the face of a difficult situation. Never again need you feel lost, confused, or dismayed—irrespective of the appearances which confront you.

There is always a glorious answer. You can use the Perfect Power within you which will bring your life and affairs into a state of balance and perfect right action.

The Five Steps in a Spiritual Mind Treatment

The five steps in a Spiritual Mind Treatment are:

1. recognition of the Perfect Power;
2. unification with the Perfect Power;
3. choosing your good;
4. accepting your good;
5. thanksgiving.

Now Let's Try It

Step No. 1—Recognition of the Perfect Power. This is the first and most important step. It cannot be overdone. It means to recognize the Power and the Presence of God right where you are and everywhere present within every part of life. Infinite Good is everywhere present. Since infinite Good is everywhere present, how can evil exist? Infinite Love is everywhere present, like a loving father, desiring your highest good, loving you with an *everlasting love* which encompasses everything that concerns you.

Divine Love is Power in your life, omnipotent Power, All-Power, a Power so great you cannot even conceive of it, a Power to which nothing is impossible. All Power includes Wisdom and Intelligence. Infinite Intelligence knows the answer to your every problem and is able to bring order and right action into your life in ways you know not of.

We recognize that the Power is the source of all good and is able to provide us not only with ideas but with the substance out of which they can be executed. It is wholeness, divine well-being which outpictures as physical and mental health and abundant supply.

If you are treating for another, realize that God is one Infinite Mind and that you are not separated from the person for whom you are treating. Furthermore, you are not trying to change the other person but you are changing your thinking about that person. The Perfect Power within you and within all of life knows how to bring perfect right action into his experience.

The *key thought* in this first step is to recognize that God is everywhere present. You cannot become separated from God (Good) for a single instant. You have only *thought* yourself separated. As we realize the Omnipresence of God, we realize that there is no place where God, infinite Good, divine Love, perfect Peace, is not. We do not have to make God happen. God already exists in fullness in every part of life. God is all-wise, all-knowing, and all-powerful and knows how to do all things for us, through us, in the right and perfect way.

Step No. 2—Unification with the Perfect Power within you. Now we know of the existence of the Perfect Power which is God. We have recognized it as being within ourselves and within all of life.

Without man, God would not be expressed, for man is the image and likeness of God. This means that as Sons of God we have right within us the Power, the Intelligence and the Love of God. It is right where we are and we are one with it. All things are possible to God *through man.*

In order to feel consciously unified with God, first surrender all of the hates, anxieties, resentments, and negative thinking, and let the oneness of God's perfect Life fill the mind. Forgive yourself and your fellow man for every past mistake. As long as we separate ourselves from another living soul, we separate ourselves from God. Think to yourself: I am one with all of Life. I love my fellow man and all of Life. I am one with the creative Power of Life. I am one with God's healing Light. I am one with God's divine Abundance. I am not separated from any part of Life. *I and the Father are one.* God is living His perfect Life through me now. All that God is I am in expression.

Step No. 3—Choosing your good. Now in this awareness of the Presence and Power of God, we take the third step which is to place into mind the desire of the heart. Be relaxed in your choosing. *It is the Father's good pleasure to give you the kingdom.* The will of God for you is for an abundant, healthful, joyful, and happy life because the will of God must conform to the nature of God and the nature of God is love, joy, and life. Suffering, lack, torment, and sorrow stem from our own ignorance and lack of understanding of God.

In making your choice for yourself or for another, turn completely away from the old condition, the ill health, or the lack of abundance, and give your attention to the new choice. In other words, *start with the answer,* rather than focusing on the problem. Think about the desired perfection. Know that this perfection exists now in the mind of God.

Just as we plant a seed in the soil, we place the desire in mind knowing that the divine Intelligence knows what to do to make it grow and bear fruit. It is important that we make a choice and stick to it. When we plant a carrot seed, we will not get a cantaloupe. We have to know what we want and then we let it come into manifestation. God knows how to bring it into our experience at the right and perfect time.

Step No. 4—The fourth step is accepting your good. This requires faith. Jesus said, *What things soever ye desire, when ye pray believe that ye receive them and ye shall have them.* This is where most people fail. They don't feel that they are worthy of accepting the good that really belongs to them. *All that the Father hath is thine.* You are indeed a *son of God,* beloved of the Father, and it is the Father's good pleasure to give you a healthy body, a happy life, and an abundance of all good things.

You need only to accept them as coming from the one Source and they are yours. That which you accept or experience in mind will become manifest in your outer experience. If your heart's desire is born in love and does not harm anyone else, then you should be able to accept it confidently.

Step No. 5—The fifth step is giving thanks for your good. Jesus gave thanks before the visible manifestation of the healing. As he stood before the tomb of Lazarus, he said, *Father, I thank Thee that Thou hast heard me,* even before he commanded Lazarus to come forth. Not only had he accepted the healing, but he was so sure that he gave thanks beforehand. The fifth step is really part of the fourth step for it is an act of faith which strengthens your acceptance to the point where you really believe that it is done and can really release the entire situation to *The Father within who doeth the works.* The fifth step is often called *the releasing.* As you give thanks—*let go and let God.*

These are the five steps in a spiritual mind treatment. They constitute scientific prayer. The same thought sequence appears in the Lord's Prayer. When properly used and understood, the five steps accomplish a complete changing of the mind or consciousness. It is like changing the slide in the projector. A new picture appears on the screen. As we change our minds through treatment, we will find our lives changing to conform to our new thought patterns. *As within, so without.*

We live in a spiritual universe and every time we treat, something is bound to happen. The idea is to persist until the mind has really become changed and can accept the new idea. As we persist, there will be a fulfillment of our heart's desires.

A Treatment for Prosperity
Using the Five Steps

I love the Lord, my God, with all my heart, my soul, and my mind. I keep my mind centered in this love for God, the source of all life. Thus I am one with the source of all good. All that the Father hath is mine. I give away all thoughts of lack, fear, and poverty. I open my mind to receive God's wonderful abundance. I am a perfect channel for the expressing of divine ideas into life. Each idea is accompanied by all that is needed to bring it into manifestation. Father means feeder, provider, protector. As I turn to the Father within, my every need is met. I am abundantly supplied with all that I can accept from an infinite Source. I accept prosperity. God's right action is my right action. I move from one joyous, prosperous experience to another. And for this I give thanks.

And so it is

A treatment for Companionship
Using the Five Steps

God is Love. God is All in all. There is no place where Love is not. God is Love and when we love we are like Him. In the measure that I love I will draw to me love and understanding. I now silently send out thoughts of love to all the world, those whom I know and those whom I do not know. I freely forgive all those who have ever hurt me. I am one with God and one with God expressed in every other person. I can never be lonely, for the love that warms my heart is the love that I give forth to life. It is wherever I am. I choose perfect friends and I know that in the one mind they exist for me. I trust God to manifest to me as friendship. I accept perfect companionship in my life. I thank Thee, Father, that this is so.

And so it is

Statement of Truth (A reminder)

Be sure to use your Statements of Truth, one for each day of the week that you are studying this lesson. Here is the way to do it:

1. Relax and be still for a few minutes.

2. Now read the Statement of Truth through at least three times.

3. In the silence, meditate on this thought for a few minutes.

4. Carry the card with you all day. Read the Statement of Truth and meditate on it as often as you can.

5. Read the Statement of Truth just before you go to sleep and go to sleep meditating on it.

LESSON SIX —

STATEMENT OF TRUTH — FIRST DAY

I Am Unified With God's Love

As I accept the fullness of God's infinite Love and become unified with it, there is no room in my consciousness for criticism, judgment, or condemnation of myself or others. I affirm all of life.

And so it is

LESSON SIX —

STATEMENT OF TRUTH — SECOND DAY

I Express Perfect God

I am the perfect expression of a perfect God. As such, I am free with the Freedom of God; at peace in the Peace of God; fulfilled in the Love of God; guided by the Wisdom of God.

And so it is

LESSON SIX —

STATEMENT OF TRUTH — THIRD DAY

I Am One With God and All of Life

I know no feeling of separation from any living soul, for we are all one in God. I send my love out to all the world and it returns to me from everyone I meet.

And so it is

LESSON SIX —

STATEMENT OF TRUTH — FOURTH DAY

I Am Confident

Confidence in the self means believing in the Perfect Power within. I trust this Perfect Power each moment of the day. I trust it for right ideas and for guidance in carrying out these ideas. I trust it in everyone.

And so it is

LESSON SIX —

STATEMENT OF TRUTH — FIFTH DAY

I Know the Perfect Power Knows

I rest in the knowledge that the Perfect Power within me knows how to function my life and affairs perfectly. God within me is my perfect health (wholeness) in mind, body, and affairs.

And so it is

LESSON SIX —

STATEMENT OF TRUTH — SIXTH DAY

I Trust the Word I Speak

I trust the word that I speak in treatment. I know that my word has power because it is coupled with the power of Infinite Mind. Infinite Mind is the knower and the doer. As I speak my word, it is clothed with all that it needs to bring it into manifestation NOW.

And so it is

LESSON SIX —

STATEMENT OF TRUTH — SEVENTH DAY

Now Is the Accepted Time

I realize that in the law of Mind there are no limitations in time or space. Now is the only time that there is. All that needs to take place is taking place right now. I relax knowing that all that needs to be done is being done easily, without strain or pressure.

And so it is

Lesson VII

DEMONSTRATING THE PERFECT POWER WITHIN

Let's See How Far We Have Come

In the first lesson we learned who we really are; that each one is an inlet and an outlet of the Perfect Power within which is the infinite Power of God.

In Lesson II we glimpsed the possibilities of choosing a new life for the self and saw that the Perfect Power within was ready and waiting to bring this new life into expression.

Lesson III showed us the importance of our beliefs; that the world in which we live is the sum total of these beliefs. As we choose new beliefs we are choosing a new life. In this third Lesson we changed a lot of beliefs and claimed our divine heritage as true sons of God.

In Lesson IV we learned how the Law works; that the thoughts which we plant in mind are like seeds which reproduce after their kind to become things in our experience.

Lesson V brought out that it is in the silence of the mind that this takes place.

Lesson VI gave us the key—treatment which releases the Perfect Power within to do its perfect work.

Now We're Ready For Results of Spiritual Mind Treatment

The results are known as demonstrations because they actually demonstrate the working of the Law of life in our experience. A demonstration is positive proof of the infallible and immutable way in which the Law works. A demonstration is answered prayer — the fruit for which the seed was planted. If you like the fruits you are receiving, rest assured you have been planting good seed thoughts. The Law keeps right on working and every experience or demonstration in our lives, be it good or bad in our judgment, is the outpicturing of the kind of thoughts we have been sowing. Thoughts are indeed things. If you do not like the kind of demonstrations you have been making, you have only to choose to plant new seeds and do it. You, alone, are making your life. You, alone, determine how you will use the Perfect Power within you. You are not at the mercy of outside conditions, circumstances, or personalities.

Demonstrations and Signs Following

Just as the seed bursts from its shell and puts down roots into the deep silence of the soil, so with us the real work takes place in the invisible world of the mind and the demonstrations which appear are the subsequent signs of which the Bible speaks: *And these signs shall follow them that believe.* We must believe so thoroughly that there will be *signs following,* that we cease to look over the shoulder to see if they are coming. To look back is the same thing as digging up the seed to see what's happening. It interferes with the creative process and stops all growth at that point. If you dig up the seed, you must start all over again and plant a new one. So it is with a treatment.

When we let doubt and uncertainty creep in, when we start anxiously fretting for the demonstration, then we must treat the situation all over again until we can release it to the Perfect Power within. *The Perfect Power within you knows how to bring about your demonstration in the perfect way at the right and perfect time.*

Start With the Answer

This is what Jesus meant when he said, *What things soever ye desire when ye pray, believe that ye receive them, and ye shall have them.* He had just gotten through giving his disciples a strong example: *Whosoever shall say unto this mountain, be thou removed, and be thou cast into the sea; and shall not doubt in his heart, but shall believe that these things which he saith shall come to pass; he shall have whatsoever he saith.* What a bold statement! The old type of prayer was to start with the problem and never get away from the problem. This resulted in digging the self in deeper and deeper. We have to turn away from the difficulty and start with the answer. Start with what you desire — *have faith in God* — believe in your desire and in the ability of the Perfect Power within you to bring it into expression. What you have faithfully believed will some day become a reality in your outer experience.

How Specific Should We Be?

Be careful what you pray for, you will get it, said Emerson. It is fine to be specific in your treatment. If you treat for a twenty-room house and believe that you will receive it, you will have it. But are you sure that you want all of the responsibility that goes with it?

I know a person who treated for one thousand dollars. To her a thousand dollars seemed like a fortune. Some time later she received exactly one thousand dollars from an estate. She was perturbed because her sister received three thousand dollars from the same estate. She actually got what she asked for. The Law is definite in its working. She would have been better off to have set no limit on the Infinite—to have treated for abundance. Sometimes we can be too specific.

God Wants You to Have the Best

Treat first for guidance. The Perfect Power within you knows what is right for you and will guide you in making wise choices. It is we who limit ourselves. Jesus said, *what things soever . . . For since the beginning of the world men have not heard, nor perceived by the ear, neither hath the eye seen, O God, beside thee, what he hath prepared for him that waiteth for him.* Isaiah said it and Paul quoted him. They both knew that the loving Father wants us to have the very best. People usually choose second best because they cannot accept more for themselves. This does not mean that one has to be greedy to get the best, but it does mean that life is not holding out on us— the more we put into life, the more life will give to us.

Love is all around us and is really a part of us, if we would but recognize its presence. Understanding and wisdom are already ours to use and share as we let them become a part of our daily experience. What is right on a spiritual plane also is right on a mental plane. I have known people to seek spiritual joy through a veil of mental tears. Their minds were filled with sadness, sorrow, and worry; they approached the idea of the spiritual life in that mental state. Sadness, sorrow, or worry never glorify God. Neither does material poverty nor physical illness. One glorifies God by letting his light shine—by living an enthusiastic, happy, radiant, and fulfilled life — by overcoming the trials and tribulations with ease and through scientific prayer or treatment. *It is the Father's good pleasure to give you the kingdom.* The will of God is always for good.

Where Does the Demonstration Take Place?

The demonstration takes place on three planes. The first plane is in the conscious mind of the person treating. The next plane is in the subconscious mind of the person treating, which is one with the Universal Subconscious Mind. *In Spirit we live and move and have our being.* The third plane is the plane of visible manifestation. This we think of as the material or physical plane. If one is treating for wisdom, it would be evidenced as wise decisions. If one is treating for the right home, it would be outpictured as the right place to live.

The important thing here is that the demonstration first takes place in the mind of the person treating and manifests in the way that would be positive proof that the demonstration has taken place.

When Does the Demonstration Take Place?

In the mind of the person treating, the demonstration has to take place *now*. Contained within the treatment is the complete demonstration. There should be no doubt about the ability of mind to bring forth the outer manifestation at the right and perfect time. There is a right and perfect time for everything to happen in this life of ours. Mind knows that right and perfect time. It has nothing to do with a clock or a calendar. The flower seed has within it all of the fragrance, the beauty, and the form of the flower. The blossom comes forth at the right and perfect time. All of these exist in the seed as a divine idea and they appear at the right time. So it is with our treatment and demonstration.

If your demonstration seems to be delayed, it is because there is something more to be done in mind. Be patient. It will become visible at the perfect, right time.

So many times, I have heard people say, "Nothing has happened that you can see but inside I feel differently." Then I know that the demonstration is bound to follow.

What Makes the Demonstration Happen?

You don't. The farmer does not make the seed grow. He does everything he can to help it by preparing the soil, cultivating the soil, adding some moisture if it is needed and keeping out the weeds. But he *releases the seed to the soil.*

When you have a treatment, release it to Mind. Do the things that need to be done, such as picking out the weeds of worry, anxiety, and doubt. Relax. Even if the one for whom you are treating is on the verge of death, worry and anxiety will not help, but affirmative, positive knowing will help more than you can possibly know.

After your treatment you may seem impelled to do some material or physical thing. If it feels right to do, go ahead and do it.

One day I needed a certain book that was out of print. I called several book stores and they told me it was impossible to get the book. Then I decided to treat. After the treatment, I dismissed the book from my mind. The next day I was in a strange city, driving down a main thoroughfare. All of a sudden, I had an urge to turn at the next corner. I did this and had driven two blocks when I saw a sign saying that a second-hand book store was selling out. I was impelled to go in. The store was filled with people. I found a clerk and asked for the book. He said they did not have it. I had an urge to look on a certain shelf and there was the book I wanted.

Here is another example. One time I treated for a woman who had been deaf for ten years. Two day later, she thought she heard the phone ring.

The next day she went to a hearing-aid specialist, was fitted, and heard perfectly. Now, here is the interesting part. Ten years before, five years before, and two years before, she had been examined by the best men in this field and they all told her she could never hear again *even with a hearing aid*. They said it was a physical impossibility. She did not accept this verdict, but believed. The hearing aid proved to be a step in the demonstration. Today, she hears well without a hearing aid. The demonstration is complete.

What Is Your Part in the Demonstration?

Do the thing that feels natural and reasonable to do. Dr. Laurence Jones, the founder of the Piney Woods School in Mississippi, who, with $2.65, started that wonderful institution that now covers hundreds of acres, said he would pray as if it all depended on God and then he would work as if it all depended on him.

Do not hesitate to take the necessary human footsteps that come easily and seem to be prompted from within. After all, God works for you through you. Just beware of trying to force the outcome. God works easily and without strain. You do not have to make anything out of anything; it already *is* in Mind.

We should not be afraid to work. It is not work that hurts us. It is the strain, stress, and conflict of assuming that it all depends on us. When you treat, you take God into partnership. Place your burdens and cares on the Lord, the divine law of life. It knows how to handle them with ease.

Outlining — What It Means

Outlining means to specify, step by step, how a demonstration should take place. We should be careful not to do this. We must know what we want and then depend on the intelligence of the Perfect Power to bring it into our experience. Trust and know that the right thing will take place at the right time. The Perfect Power within you can see around the corners and you can't. Therefore, it knows better ways than you know.

Change Is Inevitable in the Outer Experience

There is nothing so certain as change. The Perfect Power within you never changes, but the world is always changing. When one treats, one must be willing to accept change. Sometimes the changes that take place before the demonstration cause alarm — they may be so drastic. However, before a new structure can be built, you have to remove the old; before health can be restored, the old thought patterns have to be pulled up and cast out.

One must be willing to let changes be made in order for the demonstration to take place.

A Treatment for Right Decision

There is no problem, no seemingly confused situation to which the answer is not already known in the divine Mind. In truth, then, there is no problem. God is the truth in each situation, perfect right action expressing in my life. As I am made aware of the God Power expressing as rightness in my life and the lives of all whom I desire to help, all confusion clears away. Right answers, heretofore unknown to me, are revealed to me with amazing accuracy. They come from the one Mind through my point of awareness with that Mind. I find there is a perfect solution that blesses everyone. No one can be hurt when God makes the decision. As I listen to the still small voice within me, I am guided in making right decisions. The wisdom of God makes them for me and I make no mistakes. As I turn to the all-knowing Power within, the burden of responsibility slips from my shoulders and the way appears clear before me. Today and every day I will let God make right decisions for me in everything that I do.

And so it is

LESSON SEVEN —

STATEMENT OF TRUTH — FIRST DAY

I Contemplate My Heart's Desire

That which I contemplate becomes my experience. I now turn my entire attention away from the problem and contemplate my heart's desire knowing that the Perfect Power within me knows how to bring it into my experience.

And so it is

LESSON SEVEN —

STATEMENT OF TRUTH — SECOND DAY

I Am in Harmony With Life

I am in the right place doing the right thing at the right time. This is a golden moment in which I rest knowing that my good is already on the way and will become manifest at the right and perfect time.

And so it is

LESSON SEVEN —

STATEMENT OF TRUTH — THIRD DAY

I Make Right Choices

God wants me to have the best. The Perfect Power within me knows what is right for me and is guiding me into right choices.

                              And so it is

LESSON SEVEN —

STATEMENT OF TRUTH — FOURTH DAY

God's Will Is for Health

The will of God for me is health. As I think thoughts of health, I am letting the will of God be done in my body. God is healing me NOW.

                              And so it is

LESSON SEVEN —

STATEMENT OF TRUTH — FIFTH DAY

There Is Only Power in God

There is no power in conditions.
There is no power in situations.
There is no power in personalities.
There is only Power in God,
The Perfect Power within me!

And so it is

LESSON SEVEN —

STATEMENT OF TRUTH — SIXTH DAY

Nothing Is Impossible

I dare to expand my horizons. Nothing is too hard for God working in and through me. I can do all things through the Perfect Power which strengthens me.

And so it is

LESSON SEVEN —

STATEMENT OF TRUTH — SEVENTH DAY

I Believe

"Every good gift and every perfect gift cometh from above." That which I desire is stepped down into visible manifestation from the Intelligence within me. I look to the Perfect Power within me for my demonstration.

And so it is

Lesson VIII

THE PERFECT POWER HEALS —
MIND, BODY AND AFFAIRS

What Is Health?

God created man in his image and likeness and
pronounced that creation *very good*. Why, then,
is the average man and woman today beset by
all kinds of bodily ills so that he or she must be
continuously doctoring, dosing, and even operating
on the body to make it function? Has God aban-
doned his creation? Or has man separated himself from his divine source? Is health the natural
heritage of man? Or is health to be found only
as the result of taking drugs?

What is health? I believe that health is not
merely the absence of disease but is divine well-
being. I believe that it is the natural and divine
heritage of man, who is truly the image and likeness of God, created to express the perfect Source
of all Life. I believe that it is wholeness of spirit,
mind, and body.

God is *of purer eyes than to behold evil*. God is
not the author of sickness or disease, and *without
him was not anything made that was made*. If you
are not at the present moment enjoying perfect

health, which is wholeness expressed in spirit, mind, and body, you can turn at once to the Perfect Power within you and discover this divine well-being.

Life is a trinity — spirit, mind, and body. True health must be experienced on all three levels. Health, then, is first an awareness of God, a feeling of oneness with all of life and the infinite goodness of life. Next it is a mind that is free from fear, anxiety, negation, and resentment, and, lastly, a body that expresses this spiritual and mental balance as physical well-being, radiant vitality, boundless energy, the bloom of life, a true expression of the perfect Source of all Life. *Be ye perfect even as your Father in heaven is perfect.*

This is not too much to expect. No matter how far from this goal you may believe yourself to be at present, you can enjoy perfect health. There are no incurable diseases. With God nothing is impossible. By turning to the Perfect Power within you, you can experience wholeness of spirit, mind, and body.

What Is Disease?

Disease is just what it indicates, a lack of ease or well-being of mind, body, or affairs. It is safe to say that where there is dis-ease of mind there will be disease of body and affairs as well.

Doctors are more and more coming to agree that the whole man must be treated. The body and affairs are merely the parts that show. To treat symptoms is simply to temporarily alleviate the condition which will then pop out someplace else. We live in a mental world and a healthy mind produces a healthy body.

We hear a lot about psychosomatic medicine these days. The dictionary defines psychosomatic as *pertaining to both mind and body* and psychosomatic medicine as *the use of methods and principles of psychology in the treatment of physical ailments.*

Dr. Flanders Dunbar in her book, *Mind and Body,* considered to be one of the basic books in psychosomatic medicine, said that psychosomatic refers to spirit, mind, and body. The dictionary defines psyche as spirit, soul, and mind. The human soul is the subconscious mind of the individual which is the complete record, the sum total of all that that individual has ever thought, said, or done.

The body is like a sensitive barometer reflecting the thinking of the individual. There are many examples of this in our everyday experience. We have all had the experience of blushing at some inner embarrassment. A family quarrel can cause such a digestive upset as to cause those involved to become ill. Excitement causes the heart to flutter and mental irritation can bring on a rash. It is commonly accepted today that ulcers are of psychosomatic origin—*It's not what you eat but what's eating you.*

What Is Healing?

Down through the ages there have been spiritual healings. These have been considered to be *miracles*. The miracle *is* that we have so long allowed ourselves to put up with disease. When man becomes aware for even a single instant of the perfection which is God, he begins to express some of that perfection in his mind and the projection of his mind known as body. You cannot turn wholeheartedly to the Perfect Power within you and not experience healing in some degree. Healing is simply returning to the normal, natural state of divine well-being which is man's rightful heritage. The Bible states, *God is of purer eyes than to behold evil and can not look upon iniquity.* God is not aware of sin, sickness, and death. These are false concepts in the limited thinking of the little human self.

When man unifies his thinking with the Mind of God, he finds wholeness, peace, harmony, and divine right action. At this level of consciousness there is no sickness or suffering. It was a false, erroneous concept. Since it does not exist in the Mind of God, it has no reality. Our answer, then, is, through treatment, to become aware of man's true identity as a son of God. There is no sickness but a sense of separation from the perfect life of God. Unification with God is bound to bring healing or a realization of spiritual wholeness outpictured as physical health. It is we who make it seem complicated. Say to the self: "I am a divine, perfect, spiritual being, uncontaminated by sickness or suffering. The Perfect Power within me knows how to heal me and is healing me now." If you come to believe this as the truth about yourself you will be healed. It is as simple as that.

Are There Some Diseases Which Are Incurable?

Usually a person turns to God for healing after he has tried every form of cure on the physical level; after the doctors have given him up. *Man's extremity is God's opportunity,* wrote John Flavel. If you had witnessed as many healings of so-called *incurable diseases* as I have, you would agree with him completely. It is when man is forced to give up his dependence on human panaceas and human personalities that he is able to turn completely to the omnipotent Power of God *to which nothing is impossible. If thou canst believe, all things are possible to him that believes,* said Jesus. Another time he said, *If you abide in me and my words abide in you, you shall ask what ye will and it shall be done.* He meant — if you abide in my consciousness of oneness with the Father, as the Source of all perfect life, then you can call upon the Father with the same assurance that I have. *There are no incurable diseases.* There are no diseases at all in the Mind of God which, being perfect, is constantly thinking Its creation into perfect expression.

But we must abide in Love. We cannot continue to think thoughts of hate, or even criticism and resentment, nor can we be filled with fear and anxiety and expect to experience health of mind and body.

A friend of mine was given up by one of the largest medical clinics in the United States, given up to die of so-called cancer within two months. She turned to God for healing and engaged a practitioner to treat for her.

My friend, who had always been terribly afraid to be alone, overcame this fear through treatment to the extent that she was able to go away by herself and live alone in a trailer for a period of several weeks. During this time she read books on spiritual mind healing and literally *prayed without ceasing*. As a result of this prayerful activity, it came to her that her *little hates* were standing in the way of her healing.

She had never really hated anyone or anything in her life, but she said that she realized that she *hated* doing the dishes and other routine jobs around the house. She called these resistances to certain things her *little hates*. At this point she began to consciously unify with all of life, loving each part of life. She got rid of those *little hates*. She came to feel one with Life. There was no longer a sense of separation from God. When she reached this point, she was healed of the so-called incurable disease from which she had been given an ultimatum of two months to live.

For many years she enjoyed life thoroughly and shared her faith with others. She *lived* what the world calls a miracle. The doctors were astounded. To her it seemed the most natural thing in the world. *If ye abide in me, and my word abides in you, ye shall ask what ye will and it shall be done.* Our part is to abide in the Christ consciousness, Love made manifest in and through man. The Perfect Power does the rest.

There Are no Incurable Diseases— A Treatment

Let this mind be in you which was also in Christ Jesus.
Phil. 2:5.

In the One Mind there are no incurable diseases; there is only perfection of God. In the one Life there are no dangerous symptoms, difficult conditions; no pain or suffering. The awareness of the presence of God dissolves these troublesome thoughts and their seeming effects as *a light shining in a dark place.* The Christ mind is the Mind of God, the consciousness that *all power is given unto me in heaven (within) and earth (without)* and *I and my Father are one.* As I let this mind be in me, I am clothed in shining garments (spiritual thoughts) of perfection. I speak the healing word of God with the authority of the Christ. God's perfection is my perfection and shines on all that I behold. *That light that lighteth every man* illumines my world and the universe. There is only one Life, the Life of God. That Life has never been sick, never suffered, never been less than whole. That Life is my life now. For this I give thanks.

And so it is

The Power of Your Word

Your every thought has power. *Every thought is motor in its consequences,* wrote William James. And I love the statement of his brother, Henry James, *The visible world is but man turned inside out that he may be revealed to himself.*

Your every thought is reflected in your body temple. It produces after its kind. A strong, positive thought, filled with faith and love, causes one to feel warm and uplifted and sets the healing forces within the body into motion; while a thought filled with fear and anxiety produces an adverse effect on the body. Men under the stress and extreme fear of battle have been known to age twenty years in one day.

If you do not like what you are experiencing in your visible world, you can set about to change it by changing your invisible thought world.

I have set before you life and death, blessing and cursing: therefore choose life, that both thou and thy seed shall live. (Deut. 30:19) The Bible is a book of wisdom, not superstition.

This explains the story of Jesus withering the fig tree. I have known people to say they thought the story must have been misquoted, for how could Jesus have been so unloving as to wither a living tree just because it did not bear fruit for him out of season. Yet, if you take Mark's story of the incident (Mark 11:12-26), you will find that Jesus was hungry. He approached the tree in anticipation

of fruit and found only leaves. He said unto it,
No man eat fruit of thee hereafter for ever.

The next morning they again passed the tree
and Peter remembered the incident and said to
Jesus, *Master, behold, the fig tree which thou
cursed is withered away.*

What do you think was Jesus' answer? Was he
sorry, or remorseful, or compassionate toward the
tree? He said, *Have faith in God. For verily I say
unto you, that whosoever shall say unto this mountain, Be thou cast into the sea; and shall not doubt
in his heart, but shall believe that those things
which he saith shall come to pass; he shall have
whatsoever he saith.*

Jesus, the greatest of all teachers, was showing in
a colorful and provocative way that your word has
the power to raise up or to tear down; to create
or to destroy. What a vivid example!

Modern Experiments in Blessing
And Cursing

Some years ago a young Congregational min-
ister named Franklin Loehr decided that he would
experiment for himself with plants and see if blessing and cursing would actually affect them. He
set up two groups of plants, giving each identical
physical growing conditions. Each day he mentally
blessed one group and mentally cursed the other.
The group that he blessed grew much faster and
stronger than the group which was cursed. While

all of the blessed plants grew, many of the cursed ones withered and died. He tried this experiment several times, and was finally convinced that a law was at work.

He then left his pulpit and organized the Religious Research Foundation. A laboratory was set up in which thousands of experiments were conducted under test conditions. Also hundreds of seed kits for experiment were prepared and distributed to those who were curious and could conduct the experiments in their own homes. Articles have been published in several nationally-known magazines concerning these experiments. Perhaps you have read them. The results proved conclusively that blessing plants aided their growth, while cursing them caused their growth to be interfered with even though the same physical conditions prevailed.

Many of my students tried these experiments with exciting results. They came to the conclusion that the green-thumb theory has a scientific basis. It is not coincidence that people who love their gardens have such unique success with their plants.

You Can Try It Yourself

Would you like to try this experiment for yourself and thereby realize the power of your word? This is how it is done:

Prepare two flat pans with soil, the same soil, the same depth, as nearly alike as you can make

them. Now take twenty-four kernels of corn se-
lected at random. Without examining the corn,
divide the kernels into two piles. Plant one group
of twelve in one pan and the other group in the
other pan. Give them identical surroundings, the
same light, the same amount of water, but each
day mentally *talk* to one group this way:

> *I bless you and praise you for the God-life
> that is in you. The omnipotent power within you
> is making you grow. God is making you flourish,
> giving you a good solid growth. You are put-
> ting down good roots and sending up an abund-
> ant growth. All of the power that you need is
> contained right within your seed. I love you and
> bless you and glorify the Perfect Power within
> you.*

Now reject the other pan in your thoughts. Cursing does not necessarily mean to use swear words.
It means to call down evil upon something. You
will not enjoy condemning the other pan, but *talk*
to them something like this:

> *You are inferior and cut off from life. You
> are miserable, sickly, and weak. I have no love
> for you, no hope for you; wither and die. I hate
> you. I loathe you, and there is no good in you, no
> vitality in you. You will surely die.*

Give this pan the same amount of water and
light but deny it love, affection, and faith. We
found that in many cases these poor little plants

which received no love struggled valiantly to grow at first and, even after they reached a growth of an inch or more, shriveled and died.

The more feeling you put into this *cursing* and *blessing* the more dramatic will be your results. If properly done, you will see with the naked eye the difference in the growth of the two pans; but you will want to measure the roots and the leaf growth to prove to yourself the power of your word.

Do you begin to see how mind changes matter? Do you see how you might be influencing your own body and affairs by your thinking?

Try Blessing and Praising Your Body

Just as dramatic and even more thrilling are the experiments you can make.

A woman from Pasadena came to see me. She really needed help. She was thoroughly discouraged and seemed to have every known form of physical distress. As I remember, she had had several heart attacks, was suffering from gall-bladder trouble and arthritis, and had just discovered that she could add anemia to the list. As we talked she spoke often of "my bad heart," "my terrible digestion" and "my miserable stiff joints." I saw that with every thought she was condemning, yes, *cursing* her body.

If it worked with the plants, why wouldn't it work here, I thought. There was everything to be gained by starting a program of blessing and praising the body. I started her using the following meditation as a daily treatment. I told her to meditate on it as many times a day as she could, putting as much faith into it as possible. She was eager to find help and promised to faithfully follow my plan.

Here is the treatment:

I Bless My Body

"Know ye not that ye are the temple of God, and that the spirit of God dwelleth in you?"

I Cor. 3:16

I bless my body. It is the temple of God . . . pure spiritual substance. Every cell of my body is activated by divine Intelligence. Every organ in my body is regulated by the great involuntary Life within me in perfect harmonious action. Each organ in my body is a perfect part of a perfect whole — the perfect wholeness that is God expressing as me.

I bless my body and give thanks for it. It is a faithful servant provided and maintained by God to house the unique individualization of Spirit that I am. I bless my body and release it in perfect confidence to the Father within *who neither slumbers nor sleeps* in His care for me. I trust the Perfect Power within me to beat my heart, digest my food, circulate my blood and harmonize the entire action of my body. My body is the temple of God. The Spirit of God dwells within me. I thank Thee, Father, for Thy loving care.

And so it is

I released this woman from my thoughts entirely. Some months later she returned to see me. I hardly knew her. She was completely transformed. She was the picture of radiant health. Her opening remark was "I feel wonderful!" She went on to tell me that the doctors were amazed at her improvement and that a recent examination showed a perfect heart and no symptoms of any other disease.

An interesting aspect of this case was that, as the woman's body was undergoing this healing metamorphosis, her affairs underwent a similar change. She had felt tied, for some time, to a large old house that she couldn't sell. As she turned her attention away from the negative appearances in her life they seemed to fall away. The right buyer appeared to buy her house and she and her husband were able to buy a new, smaller house that was exactly right for them.

In Spirit we live and move and have our being. A recognition of this truth is healing in mind, body, and affairs. They are all part of each other. When there is a lift in the consciousness, there is bound to be a corresponding improvement in health circumstances.

Many people have been healed through the use of the foregoing treatment. Try it and see for yourself what a wonderful demonstration can be yours.

No matter how long you have suffered, no matter how serious the ailment is considered, nothing is impossible to God. You can be healed by the Perfect Power within you.

LESSON EIGHT —

STATEMENT OF TRUTH — FIRST DAY

I Bless My Body

I bless my body. It is wonderfully planned for my use in this life. Every cell in my body is activated by Divine Intelligence. Every organ in my body is synchronized into a perfect harmonious whole. I bless every activity of my body.

And so it is

LESSON EIGHT —

STATEMENT OF TRUTH — SECOND DAY

I Praise the Good in Others

Whenever I think of another person, I praise the good in him. As I praise the good in him, I cause that good to multiply and he is raised up. Through praising others, I am also raised up to a new awareness of Infinite Good.

And so it is

LESSON EIGHT —

STATEMENT OF TRUTH — THIRD DAY

I Am Now Healed

Perfect health is my birthright. I surrender all mental confusion, anxiety, and fear to the Perfect Power within me, which knows how to heal my body. I am now healed.

And so it is

LESSON EIGHT —

STATEMENT OF TRUTH — FOURTH DAY

God Lives Through Me

There is no sickness but a sense of separation from God. I am a divine, perfect, spiritual being and my body is the physical instrument created and maintained by the Perfect Power within.

And so it is

LESSON EIGHT —

STATEMENT OF TRUTH — FIFTH DAY

God's Love Thrills Me

I am thrilled by the feeling that God's Love lives through me making me whole and perfect. Because I see God even in my finger tips, I realize that His Perfection living through me is all that is real. My consciousness of His Presence is the only Reality in life.

And so it is

LESSON EIGHT —

STATEMENT OF TRUTH — SIXTH DAY

There Is Only One Life

There is only one Life, the Life of God. That Life has never been sick, never suffered, never been less than whole. That Life is my life now.

And so it is

LESSON EIGHT —

STATEMENT OF TRUTH — SEVENTH DAY

I Let Go and Let God

I bless my body and release it in perfect confidence to the great involuntary Life within me which knows how to make it function perfectly. I let go and let God.

And so it is

Lesson IX

THE PERFECT POWER WITHIN
MEETS EVERY HUMAN NEED

Let's Get Down to Cases

Now that you have studied the preceding lessons
and have used the spiritual exercises provided by
the Statements of Truth, you are already consciously using the Perfect Power within you and
should be experiencing demonstrations. Perhaps
you are not aware of it but the whole climate of
your thinking has been undergoing a subtle change
and your body and affairs are beginning to mirror
this change.

However, there may be some specific situation in
your life that you would like to overcome or you
may, at this point, wish to help others with their
problems.

For this reason I am presenting some specific
case histories and the treatments used to meet and
overcome these problems through the Perfect
Power within. Although the names have been
withheld, these are all true stories in the lives of

real people. Many of them are modern-day miracles. You, too, can expect miracles in your life. Nothing is impossible to the Perfect Power within you. The light of Truth always dispels the darkness of false beliefs. There is no power in conditions — there is only Power in God.

Treating for Another

When you treat for yourself, you naturally know for whom the word of Truth is spoken. When you treat for another, it is well to specify in your treatment the name of the person for whom the word is spoken.

When you treat, think, "This word is spoken for.............................." This does not mean that the word is sent. The healing takes place first in the mind of the one treating. This simply identifies the person in the one Mind. If you are called upon to treat for someone whose name you do not know, say to yourself, "the name of this person is already known to infinite Intelligence." Always unify yourself with the person for whom you are treating. You are all one in the one mind which each is privileged to use at his own point of awareness. It makes no difference how far away the one is for whom you are treating. You are all one in the one Mind which each is privileged to use at his own point of awareness. It makes no difference how far away the one is for whom you are treating. There is no distance in the one Mind.

Healing of Cancer

I received this report over the telephone which I quote in part: "Remember about two years ago you treated, at my request, for a young man who was in the Naval Hospital? He was suffering from cancer of both legs and the doctors gave him only a short time to live and wanted to amputate both legs immediately. At this time he and his wife became deeply interested in studying about the Perfect Power within and read as much as they could. That was two years ago. They did not have to amputate his legs and today I have a letter saying he and his family now are living in Alabama and he had a miraculous healing. He has a good job as a car salesman and they have had another child since he was released from the hospital."

Treatment Used in this Case

There is nothing impossible to God. All things are possible to Him. The infinite Love of God is greater than any condition. God is working through the doctors and nurses to help this man but God is the real healer. Of myself I do nothing; the Father within, He doeth the works. This man is a perfect, divine, spiritual being. His body is made of pure spiritual substance. He is one with God and God is one with him. Right now the healing Presence of God is cleansing him, healing him of any seeming imperfection. God's infinite Love neutralizes all fear and uncertainty, all bitterness and hate. God's Love permeates every part of his life and being. He is made whole and perfect now. I accept this perfect healing now. I thank God to Whom this physical perfection is already

known. In the Mind of God he has never been less than
perfect. Therefore this healing has already taken place
in the Mind of God.

And so it is

Peace of Mind

Are you one of those people who cannot put
his finger on any specific problem but constantly
goes through life with a worried, uneasy feeling?
Are you afraid of tomorrow without knowing why?
The following treatment has brought peace of
mind to many people who previously had this un-
certain feeling holding them back from their true
expression.

*I came that ye might have life and have it more
abundantly.* Life is to be lived, fully and completely, exuberantly and joyously. Let's begin today
in the quiet of the mind.

In the Quiet of the Mind

In the quiet of the mind I find the peace that passeth
all understanding. The infinite Presence of God filling
every part of life is centered within me — my Creator, the
Perfect Power of life. It expresses itself into every part
of my life right this moment. The infinite Intelligence within me knows what is right for me, makes my decisions and
tells me what to say and do moment by moment. In the
peace and quiet of my mind I realize that God is my
supply and that the spiritual substance within me provides
all that I need. Divine love in and through me out-pictures
as friends and companions wherever I go. As I meditate

on the Presence of God within me, letting my requests be made known, my life is formed and my needs are met. In the quiet of the mind, at the very center of my being, I find the peace that passeth all understanding.

And so it is

Protection When Traveling

A couple recently returned from an extended vacation to report to me that they had had a wonderful sense of protection on their trip. They said that it was almost miraculous the way they found just the right place to stay each night. Even though they drove so late that the motels appeared to be full, there was always a room waiting for them at the end of their day's journey. They said they did not even see an accident during the entire trip. Several times they preceded cloudbursts and hurricanes by a few hours and felt each time that they had been divinely protected, their timing was so perfect. "Everything worked out so perfectly, we couldn't have planned it that well ourselves," they said. They told me that they had started each day by meditating on the following treatment I had given them:

Vacation Meditation

Be strong and of a good courage; be not afraid, neither be thou dismayed: for the Lord thy God is with thee whithersoever thou goest.

Joshua 1:9

I am not alone. Wherever I am—God is. Wherever
I go, I go with God. Should traveling be in order, I have
no fear for His love goes before me and prepares the way.
Right lodging and perfect means await me as I need them.
I dedicate both my car and the trip to God. His hand is
on the wheel and His wisdom assures the smooth operation of the car. His love reaches out to help me through
everyone I meet. Each mile of the way is a glorious
adventure in the practice of the presence of God. How
can I feel lonely or apprehensive with His promise sing-
ing in my heart—*Whithersoever thou goest, I will go with
thee.* I am not alone. The Perfect Power goes with me
to be my companion and my protection each moment of
the day. I am never away from *home* when I dwell in
the house of the Lord.

And so it is

Making Decisions

I was talking to a man who had always had
trouble making decisions. In fact, he used to try
to get me to make them for him. Now, having
discovered the Perfect Power within, he has learned
to listen to the still small voice of infinite Intelligence within. He receives his guidance from the
inner Self and this gives him a sense of confidence
and security. As we discussed this remarkable
change in him, he said to me, "You know, anyone
can do this who is willing to trust the teacher within. I treat, and then I listen, and something tells
we what to do."

Treatment for Guidance In Making Decisions

Trust in the Lord with all thine heart,
And lean not unto thine own understanding.
In all thy ways acknowledge Him;
And he shall direct thy paths.

Proverbs

There is no problem, no seemingly confused situation, to which the answer is not already known to divine Mind. Infinite Intelligence knows what to do and how to do it and clears all confusion away. Right answers, heretofore unknown to me, are revealed to me with amazing accuracy. They come from the one Mind through my point of awareness with that Mind. I find there is a perfect solution to every difficulty, a solution that blesses everyone. No one can be hurt when God makes the decision. As I listen to the still small voice within me, I am guided in making right decisions. The wisdom of God makes them for me and I make no mistakes. As I turn to the all-knowing Power within me, the burden of responsibility slips from my shoulders and the way appears clear before me. In all my ways I acknowledge the Perfect Power within and it directs my paths.

And so it is

Nothing Is Ever Lost in the Divine Mind

Have you ever had a telephone call from someone who has just lost several thousand dollars—the life savings of the family? Would you be tempted to join them in their panic? You need not fear. You can assure the person calmly, "Nothing is ever lost in divine Mind." Here is a dramatic story that proves it:

The call came on a Friday morning as I was meditating in my study. The woman was nearly hysterical and I had a difficult time piecing the story together. She had been on her way to an escrow company after having cashed $2,000 in bonds at the bank. She had this money in her billfold which she carried in her purse. She made several stops on the way. At the last stop, she realized that the billfold was not in her purse. She immediately called me.

"I have already retraced my steps," she said, "and it's not to be found."

"All right, now," I said, "I want you to sit down and be still while I have a good treatment for you. There is nothing lost in divine Mind. The perfect Intelligence within you will tell you where that money is."

I used a treatment for her similar to this one:

Nothing is Ever Lost in the Divine Mind

Everything that has ever been or ever will be is known in the Mind of God. My mind is one with the Mind of God and the things that I need to know will be revealed to me at the time that I need to know them. This money is identified in the one Mind with this person to whom it belongs. Divine Love is protecting this money for the rightful owner. Divine Intelligence is revealing to her its exact whereabouts. She now quietly and serenely opens her mind to receive the necessary information. The Perfect Power within her inspires her to do whatever is needed to regain her rightful possession. I trust the Perfect Power within all of life to cooperate in bringing about divine justice in this situation. Nothing is ever lost in divine Mind. And for this I give thanks.

And so it is

What happened next? The result was even more dramatic than I had anticipated. The phone rang and a calm and happy voice gave me the outcome. After she called me the first time, she had retraced her steps twice. The second time she recalled a stop which she had not previously remembered. She had stopped at a department store merely to ask a question. To her knowledge she had not even opened her purse. But there it was, her unopened billfold, money intact, right in the entrance to the department store with hundreds of people walking over it.

Nothing is *ever* lost in the Divine Mind. All of life cooperates with the one who trusts in the Perfect Power within.

Using It in the Little Things

One day I lost my date book. That is, it seemed to be lost. Several days went by and I became tempted to feel concerned, because without it I had no way of knowing the various speaking engagements which I had made far into the future. "Now this is silly," I thought, "infinite Intelligence within me knows exactly where that book is." I was sitting in my automobile at the time and it was as if someone took my hand and guided it right under the front seat of the car where I instantly felt my leather date book. Why hadn't I thought to look there before? *I had been depending on myself to find it.* When I turned to the Perfect Power the answer was quick and direct.

Your business is God's business. Your life is God's Life. There is nothing too insignificant to take up with the Perfect Power.

Business Difficulties

A real estate man called me one day and presented a discouraging picture. "Things have just dried up," he said. "Nothing is moving at all." He went on in this vein, "I've talked to the fellows up and down the street and they all say business is bad everywhere."

"Wait a minute," I said, and proceeded to point out to him that he alone was making his life and that circumstances had no control over him. I told him that if he would turn the problem over to the Perfect Power within, ideas would come to him; if he would open his mind to receive new business, it would come to him. I suggested that he open his office each morning with the following meditation:

This is God's Business

The Lord will perfect that which concerneth me. Ps. 138.8

This business is God's business. Everything God does is done easily, smoothly, and happily. Everyone who needs to know us is being drawn to us easily so that we may help them. We give service, God's service. Love is our theme. It permeates this office and is felt by everyone who crosses our doorstep. It blesses us and all who contact us. It returns to us as happy clients and successful transactions that bless and please everyone. Those whom we can best serve are being drawn to us now. There are no depressions in the Mind of God. The Infinite knows no lack. I refuse to accept poor business — God's business is always good business.

And so it is

About two weeks later this same man got in touch with me to tell me that he had four deals in escrow and that as far as he was concerned, "Business is very good."

Right Employment

Each person is a unique individualization of Spirit. Therefore, there is a right and perfect expression for everyone. This right and perfect expression deserves the right and perfect remuneration. *The workman is worthy of his hire.* Time and again I have seen persons with seemingly everything against them—age, handicaps, lack of experience, etc., find perfect employment for their unique talents through using a treatment similar to this:

Treatment for Right Employment

God is Love and that Love expresses through me as service to others. There is perfect employment for me. God is abundance and this Abundance is my supply. As I serve life, life rewards me generously. I trust God to meet my every need. God is infinite Intelligence and this Intelligence expresses through me as guidance. As I turn to the perfect Intelligence within me, I am guided to do the right thing in the right way. My perfect employment is seeking me now. My desire to work is my prayer answered. As I take the human footsteps which are presented to me as ideas from within, I become unified with my perfect employment. In the one Mind I am one with my new employer and my perfect position right now. All anxiety is removed from this situation for I trust God to provide the perfect way to express His perfect Life through me. I give thanks for the abundance that is mine.

And so it is

The Basis for a Happy Marriage

It has often been said, "The family that prays together, stays together." This surely is true. During my ministry I have counselled with many couples who were able to save their marriages through an understanding of Truth. But the following case stands out in my mind.

This particular couple had become desperately unhappy. The wife already had purchased her ticket to "go home to mother." The one thing in their favor was a desire on the part of each one to save the marriage.

I told each one of them separately to go home and make a list of all the things they liked about the other and then to make another list of all of the things that they would like to like about the other. Then each one was to set a time aside each day to read the first list and bless the marriage partner for the various things which already were recognized values. Then each was to take the second list and bless the marriage partner for all the things that he or she wished the other had, as if they already had them. For example, if there seemed to be a lack of integrity, they were to say: "For the wonderful God-given integrity within you, I bless you and bless you."

It worked like a charm and I'll tell you why. It is a law of life that whatever you bless increases and multiplies. Marriage to be complete must first be spiritual. Marriage that is happy is not 50-50 giving but 100 percent giving. When two people bless and affirm the other, they are bound to be happy.

Treatment for a Happy Marriage

Marriage, to be complete, must first be spiritual. From this inner state of conscious unity in thought, purpose, plan, and action, there comes the outer state corresponding to it, making the outer like the inner, peaceful and harmonious. I share my own inner peace and joy with my marriage partner. My happy marriage reflects the unity within my own mind. That which we give away we keep. I give completely and unreservedly all that I have into my marriage. I am secure in my marriage. The Love of God protects us, guides us, and provides for us abundantly. I am loyal to my marriage partner and my marriage partner is loyal to me. We are one. God is loving me through my marriage partner now.

And so it is

LESSON NINE —

STATEMENT OF TRUTH — FIRST DAY

My Business Is God's Business

Infinite Intelligence within controls and maintains this business. Every idea needed for its success is abundantly supplied from an Infinite Source.

And so it is

LESSON NINE —

STATEMENT OF TRUTH — SECOND DAY

Divine Love Protects Our Family

Our family is a divine idea in the Mind of God. In God's Love we live and move and have our being. The Love of God protects us, guides us, and provides for us at all times.

And so it is

LESSON NINE —

STATEMENT OF TRUTH — THIRD DAY

I Am Always Rightfully Employed

I do not accept unemployment or lack of gainful employment in my experience. I am always in the right place at the right time doing the right thing. I am always employed in doing creative work that is right and perfect for my talents. I am always receiving right and perfect remuneration. I am happy in my work.

And so it is

LESSON NINE —

STATEMENT OF TRUTH — FOURTH DAY

I Do Not Contend With Life

I do not contend with anyone. I do not argue with anyone. I know that as I agree with my adversary quickly, all barriers of contention and separation quickly disappear. I am one with all life.

And so it is

LESSON NINE —

STATEMENT OF TRUTH — FIFTH DAY

I Reveal the Truth—God Heals

I realize that finite man is small indeed, but that God in man is Infinite. I consciously reveal the Truth about myself or the person for whom I am treating. God heals.

And so it is

LESSON NINE —

STATEMENT OF TRUTH — SIXTH DAY

I Stay in Perfect Health

Quietly and with a sense of divine assurance, I declare my immunity to disease and injury. Through Love, I harmonize with all of Life. Germs, discordant thoughts, fear, or worry have no power over me. I accept health, wholeness, and perfect action, NOW.

And so it is

LESSON NINE —

STATEMENT OF TRUTH — SEVENTH DAY

I Am Thankful

I am thankful that the Perfect Power within me illumines my path and I am reaping a rich harvest of new ideas. I am prosperous because the abundance of the Perfect Power is mine to use, NOW.

And so it is

Lesson X

LOVE IS THE FULFILLING
OF THE LAW

Love Is the Answer

Love is the answer to our every need. It makes no difference what that need may be—Love is the answer.

Love can heal a sick body; love can make friends out of enemies; love can cause a failing business to prosper. Love can erase all crime, conflict, and war from the world.

There is no condition — no matter how fixed and intolerable — which cannot be overcome by love. There is no person, regardless of what depths he has sunk to, who cannot be helped, improved, and lifted up by love.

Man, since time began, has been looking for a panacea, a universal remedy, or a cure-all for his bodily ills and for world problems. There is such a panacea. It is Love which is the Perfect Power within you. Love, properly understood, is the magic key to the kingdom of heaven within. Nothing is impossible to love. It is, in truth, the answer to every human need. *God is Love and all things are possible to God.*

What Is Love?

It is as impossible to define Love as it is to define the Infinite—for Love is the Infinite.

Love is the highest emotion or feeling that man can experience. Yet, this is just one tiny facet of Love. Love is the energy which created the universe. Love is omnipresent (everywhere present), omnipotent (all powerful), and omniscient (all knowing).

Love is God affirming His creation and calling it good; never condemning, never denying the existence of good and only good. Love continually forgives.

Love is the unlimited Power of the universe that transcends every other seeming power. Love is Spirit pouring itself out unstintingly into its creation and yet never being used up. Love is God expressing as pure feeling through the hearts of men.

We love because He first loved us. Our love must always be a finite concept of this great all-embracing Love. Every time we think love or express love we become unified with the great power of love, we *become like Him . . . for we see Him as He is.* Like everything else the word God means to us, Love is there for us to use that we may share in His glory.

God is love and he who abides in love abides in God, and God abides in him (I Jn. 4:16). If God is Love, why do we have violence, sickness,

and suffering in this world of ours? The answer
is we are creatures of choice, so if we want love
and its effects, we must choose love. Every time
we hate, condemn, or even mildly criticize another;
every time we fear or in any way trust in a power
opposed to love, we are separating ourselves from
the God of Love and we experience the resulting
misery of that separation. When we do this we are
like the prodigal son who chose to go to a far
country, for we, too, leave the Father's house (consciousness of Love) and must suffer the consequences.

*There is no fear in love, but perfect love casts
out fear. For fear has to do with punishment, and
he who fears is not perfected in love.* (I Jn. 4:18).

Love One Another

Jesus gave us this Commandment, *love one
another.* And John, his beloved disciple, pointed
out later, *If any one says, I love God, and hates
his brother, he is a liar; for he who does not love
his brother whom he has seen, cannot love God
whom he has not seen.*

I like Dr. Harry Overstreet's definition of love
from his book, *The Mature Mind.* He said, *The
love of a person implies, not the possession of that
person, but the affirmation of that person. It
means granting him, gladly, the full right to his
unique humanhood. One does not truly love a*

*person and yet seek to enslave him—by law or by
bonds of dependency and possessiveness.*

Jesus, the great wayshower, admonished us,
*Love your enemies, bless them that curse you,
do good to them that hate you, and pray for them
who despitefully use you and persecute you.*

William Lyon Phelps once wrote, *How can I
love my enemies? Even many orthodox church
members do not take these words of Jesus
seriously. But as a matter of fact, the command
to love our enemies is eminently practical. It is
a remedy for a mental disease, the remedy for our
health and well-being. We must eliminate from
our minds the poison of hate.*

How Important Is Love?

Paul, who had such an excellent working knowledge of the law, called love, *the still more excellent way.* He said:

*If I speak in the tongues of men and of
angels, but have not love, I am a noisy gong
or a clanging cymbal. And if I have prophetic
powers, and understand all mysteries and all
knowledge, and if I have all fatih, so as to
remove mountains, but have not love, I am
nothing. If I give away all that I have, and if
I deliver my body to be burned, but have not
love, I gain nothing.*

I Cor. 13:1-3. (Revised Standard Version).

Paul was saying, in essence, I may speak with the oratorical genius of an Ingersoll or the logical simplicity of a Lincoln, or with the wisdom of a Plato, but, if I have not love, I am merely a loud, discordant noise. I may uncover, understand, and use the secrets of atomic energy or I may have such faith in myself and the laws of nature that I could overcome obstacles that seem like mountains. Or I may be a great benefactor and give away millions of dollars or I may be a martyr to some cause and give up my life for it. *But if I do not have love, all of these would count for nothing.*

Paul went on further to say this about love, *Love is patient and kind; love is not jealous or boastful, it is not arrogant or rude. Love does not insist on its own way; it is not irritable or resentful; it does not rejoice at wrong, but rejoices in the right. Love bears all things, believes all things, hopes all things, endures all things. Love never ends.*

Love Is the Fulfilling of the Law

The law of cause and effect always works perfectly and in accord with the direction given it. Our experiences of today are the fruits of the seed thoughts which we planted yesterday. If we do not like these experiences we must be careful to make wiser choices in the future. If the expe-*riences of today do not seem to be loving, then our* underlying motive has somewhere along the line not been one of love. We reap exactly what we sow. Love begets love and hate begets hate. *With what measure ye mete, it shall be meted to you again.* If every motive were based on love we would find ourselves completely fulfilled in our life experience. We could not then make a mistake. Our choices would be good choices and the results, or effects, thoroughly satisfying. Love is the Power of the universe and when we love we are one with that Power. Love is the Perfect Power within us. When we are not in harmony with Love, we are struggling against the very essence of life, battling our way upstream. Everything seems to go against us. "Why aren't my prayers answered?" we cry. Lacking love, we continue to ask amiss.

Love Depends Upon You

The question is often asked, "How can I love him? Why! I don't even *like* him!" This situation is not uncommon. Love depends not upon the attributes of the love object but upon your ability to love. You may not like what another does but you can love him. It will only hurt *you* if you hate or resent him. Your health and mental well-being, as well as your prosperity, depend upon your ability to love. I am going to make a bold statement. *There never has been or never will be an instance in the history of man where hate is justifiable or beneficial to man.* It is destructive beyond our power to imagine.

"But how can I love someone whose actions

I do not approve of?" you ask. The answer is simple. When you love, you will begin to understand why he does the things he does. This does not mean that you condone what he has done, but through love you have compassion for him. *There, but for the grace of God, go I.*

So often people think, *I'll love you if you love me.* The tendency, then is to mete out love carefully, a little at a time, in order to be sure that the same amount of love is received; in order to protect the self and be sure that one does not get hurt. Real love must be given away without claim or prejudice. *That which we give away we keep.* The only love you can ever experience is the love that you give away. Do not be afraid to give it generously. It comes from an infinite Source within.

T. L. C. Prescribed

Many doctors today are prescribing T.L.C., *Tender Loving Care,* for their patients. They are finding it the most effective medicine they can use. Even though all of the physical comforts of the patient are provided, without T.L.C. there is something lacking.

A baby does not live by milk alone. No less essential to healthy growth, and even to life itself is mother love. Thus starts an interesting article in Time Magazine. Psychoanalyst Rene A. Spitz made a 20-minute film entitled "Grief" in which the key figures were 91 infants in a foundling home in Latin-America.

It was an old, established home, well-equipped and, by all material standards, well run. Its 91 infant inmates had plenty of good food, clothing, light and air, and toys. Competent nurses fed and bathed them regularly. Only one thing was lacking: the nurses, each with 10 children to care for, were too busy to stop and play with their charges. "Each infant had the equivalent of one tenth of a mother," Dr. Spitz said, "and this was not enough."

Checking on what became of the motherless foundlings, Dr. Spitz found that no fewer than 27 (or 30 per cent) died in their first year of life, and 21 who survived their time in the home were already so scarred by life that they could only be classed as idiots. Unfortunately, he could get no data on the survival or emotional response of the 32 who were placed with foster parents. Those who died, said Dr. Spitz, suffered a gradual breakdown under stress, beginning with loss of appetite and sleeplessness, and ending with inability to withstand even minor ailments. Love starved, they were crippled in the battle for life.

Just as with the plant experiments in Lesson VIII, people must have love to blossom and grow.

Treat in Love

A spiritual mind treatment is an act of love. You are opening the way for love to come into a situation where love has been absent before. That is the reason for the treatment. Right when love comes in, the healing takes place. Love unifies and draws together all of the good. Love causes a new feeling to come into the body and the body responds by being healed.

Whenever you treat, think, "This treatment is spoken in love." And then think of how God can heal anything, because He created everything and knows all things. Then think, "The God of Love is healing him or her now."

Perfect Love Casts Out Fear

Why does the Bible tell us, *perfect love casts out fear?* Have you ever tried fearing someone whom you truly love? I do not mean the possessive kind of love one finds in a mixed-up triangle situation but real love which gives and asks nothing in return. *Love possesses not nor would it be possessed; for love is sufficient unto love,* wrote Kahlil Gibran in The Prophet.

Stop and analyze your feelings the next time you are tempted to be critical and resentful of another. Is it not that you are just a little bit afraid that that person will in some way replace you or inhibit your freedom? Hate is a bonfire that scorches the ground it burns on. Fear and resentment hurt only the one who harbors them. They are costly intruders. Let perfect love cast out fear and you will begin to lead a healthy, happy, and prosperous life.

How to Love

Time and again I have had people come to me and say, "I agree with all that you say, but now how do you love?"

In the first place, Do *you* love *yourself?* I do not mean that one be conceited and thinks that he is better than another. When you understand that God is within, then when you love God, you are loving yourself—not the little finite self, but the divine, spiritual Self. Yet, it is still YOU. Jesus said, *Love thy neighbor as thyself.* Think of who you really are, a divine, perfect, spiritual being, made in the image and likeness of God. Only when you have been able to love the Lord, thy God, at the center of your own being, can you then love your neighbor.

You have to make a conscious start to love yourself or to love another. It does not just come naturally. Think to yourself, "I love the Lord, my God, at the center of my being. I love the love of God within me." And to learn to love another, think, "I love my neighbor (speak his name). I understand him. I bless and praise him. I am one with him and he is one with me." In other words, one has to think love in order to love.

After thinking love, then express love by being loving, kind, thoughtful, considerate — not just some of the time, but all of the time. This is how we teach others. Our children see us and they follow our example.

To really love, one must live the love principle. By this I mean to cast out all thoughts of hate, fear, or resentment about another. Be consistent in the love approach. It is the only way to live and really enjoy life.

A Treatment for a Greater Awareness of Love

LOVE is the Perfect Power within me and everywhere present within all of life. *LOVE* heals, protects, and guides. *LOVE* makes the plants grow and keeps everything in the universe in balance. *LOVE* is with me always. *LOVE* goes before me and makes the crooked places straight. *LOVE* is the key to happiness, health, and prosperity for *LOVE* unlocks the kingdom of heaven within from which they proceed. Just as electricity, which has always existed in the world, must be generated before it can be used, so *LOVE* must be generated in the heart before it can be used. I generate *LOVE* from an infinite Source every time I consciously give it forth.

Every problem in my life is an opportunity to give forth more *LOVE*. If people seem to be difficult, I silently bless them until even enemies become friends—friends who have caused me to experience more *LOVE*. If there seems to be a lack in my life, I will realize more *LOVE* there, the one true substance out of which the world and its effects are made. I love and bless that which I have and silently give thanks as I watch it multiply. If I need more strength or a physical healing, the Perfect Power of *LOVE* at the center of my being will provide it. There is no sickness, no weakness, but a sense of separation from this Power. I love my body and give thanks for it. I bless the strength that I have and lo! it increases.

I call forth more *LOVE* by giving it to God and my world and this *LOVE* meets my every need.

I love God, I love my own individual expression of God, and I love my neighbor in every part of the world. There is no problem that love cannot heal. And for this I am most grateful.

And so it is

LESSON TEN —

STATEMENT OF TRUTH — FIRST DAY

I Am Prospered in Love

Love is the substance out of which everything is made. There is no lack but my lack
of Love. I accept more Love and Love pros-
pers me in a wonderful way.

And so it is

LESSON TEN —

STATEMENT OF TRUTH — SECOND DAY

My Security Is in God

My security is in God, an inner condition
that is not affected by outer circumstances.
As I turn to the Perfect Power within me
every need is met and I am secure.

And so it is

LESSON TEN —

STATEMENT OF TRUTH — THIRD DAY

I Trust the Perfect Power

"The Lord will perfect that which concerneth me." The divine Law of Life is constantly at work perfecting that which concerns me. I trust the Perfect Power within to bring divine right action into my life and affairs.

And so it is

LESSON TEN —

STATEMENT OF TRUTH — FOURTH DAY

The Love of God Blesses Me

Happiness is an inward feeling which always appears when love is shared. It does not depend upon outer circumstances but wells up in the heart, a gift of the Perfect Power within. The love I give away today returns to bless me.

And so it is

LESSON TEN —

STATEMENT OF TRUTH — FIFTH DAY

Love Is the Answer

Love is the answer to my every need. The problems in my life are simply opportunities to give forth more love. As I pour love on each situation, the problems all become answers.

And so it is

LESSON TEN —

STATEMENT OF TRUTH — SIXTH DAY

Love Takes Away All Sickness

"If thou wilt love the Lord, thy God, He will take away all sickness from thee." I love the Lord, my God, the Perfect Power within me with all my mind and with all my strength, and with all my heart. There is no room in me for fear or anxiety and I am made whole.

And so it is

LESSON TEN —

STATEMENT OF TRUTH — SEVENTH DAY

Love Is the Answer to World Peace

Love is the answer to world peace. Through Love I let peace begin with me. I send my Love forth to all the world. This thought of Love is reflected from one to another until I cannot even conceive of the blessing that started with me. Let there be peace and let it begin with me.

And so it is

ABOUT THE AUTHORS

For more than forty years, the Addingtons have worked closely together in the fields of writing and lecturing.

Jack Addington attended the University of Florida at Gainesville, and has had three successful careers, first in business where he was a practicing attorney, then twenty years in the ministry, founding two large churches. In 1969 he retired from the church to begin his worldwide ministry.

Cornelia Addington attended the University of Washington in Seattle where she majored in painting and design. She was successful as a designer for a large manufacturing firm, later going into interior design. During the past forty years, she has edited Dr. Addington's manuscripts and co-authored six of his books. She was the editor of the Abundant Living magazine and has had numerous articles published in national magazines.

Addington Books